W9-CJK-242

WITHDRAWN

1/29

SPACE PEOPLE FROM A-Z

SPACE EXPLORATION

SPACE PEOPLE FROM A-Z

**Ray Spangenburg
and
Diane Moser**

Facts On File
New York • Oxford • Sydney

Space People from A-Z

Facts On File, Inc.   Facts On File Limited   Facts On File Pty Ltd
460 Park Avenue South   Collins Street   Talavera & Khartoum Rds
New York NY 10016   Oxford OX4 1XJ   North Ryde NSW 2113
USA   United Kingdom   Australia

Library of Congress Cataloging-in-Publication Data
Spangenburg, Ray, 1939-
    Space people from A-Z / Ray Spangenburg and Diane Moser.
      p. cm. — (Space exploration ; bk. 4)
    Includes bibliographical references.
    Summary: Capsule biographies of significant individuals in the
  history of space exploration.
    ISBN 0-8160-1851-0 (alk. paper)
      1. Astronauts—Biography—Juvenile literature. [1. Astronauts.
  2. Astronautics—Biography.] I. Moser, Diane.
  II. Title. III. Series: Spangenburg, Ray, Space exploration; 4.
  TL789.85.A1S73 1990
  629.45'0092'2—dc20
  [B]
  [920]
  89-23313

British and Australian CIP data available on request from Facts On File.

Facts On File books are available at special discounts when
purchased in bulk quantities for businesses, associations,
institutions or sales promotion. Please contact the Special
Sales Department of our New York office at 212/683-2244
(dial 800/322-8755 except in NY, AK, or HI):

Text design by Ron Monteleone
Jacket design by Ron Monteleone
Composition by Facts On File, Inc.
Manufactured by the Maple-Vail Book Manufacturing Group
Printed in the United States of America

10 9 8 7 6 5 4 3 2 1

This book is printed on acid-free paper.

CONTENTS

PREFACE

Not so long ago the idea of sending anything beyond Earth's gravity was the dream of only a few rocket pioneers and visionaries. To most people the idea of humans going into space was even more outlandish. Today both feats have been accomplished. Literally hundreds of satellites encircle the Earth; people from many countries have spent time living and working in space; and, as we write this, two newly launched spacecraft, Magellan and Galileo, are heading for neighboring planets to find out more about the Solar System we live in.

Space may well be humanity's final frontier, the last and ultimate region for exploration. Unquestionably, it challenges our ingenuity, our engineering expertise, our wisdom and our courage. Above all, it tests our spirit of survival.

SPACE EXPLORATION is a series of four books that follows humankind's adventures in space. *Space People from A to Z* sketches the contributions of more than 260 of those who have made these adventures possible or taken part in them as travelers in space. Here you will find the names and stories of astronauts and cosmonauts, engineers and scientists, politicians and military officers. Each has made an important contribution: from the first sketches and calculations about rockets made by men like Konstantin Tsiolkovsky and Robert Goddard to the most recent space missions made by the men and women who fly aboard the U.S. Shuttle or travel to the Mir space station. Other books in this series tell other parts of the saga of space exploration: the story of the first space scientists, test pilots, and early astronauts and cosmonauts, including the Apollo missions to the Moon (*Opening the Space Frontier*); the continuing drama of space exploration and commercialization today, including missions aboard the first Soviet space stations called Salyut, the first U.S. space station, Skylab, the U.S. Space Shuttle and the Soviet space station Mir, as well as development of satellites and a glimpse into the future of manned space exploration (*Living and Working in Space*); and a close look at the mysteries of the Solar System uncovered by planetary probes like the Voyager, VEGA, and Viking missions (*Exploring the Reaches of the Solar System*).

Together these books tell an exciting tale of human intelligence at its best—dreaming dreams, solving problems and achieving results. We owe much to those, both past and present, who have dedicated their efforts and their lives—both personally, in manned programs, and intellectually, through their technological achievements—to venture into space.

ACKNOWLEDGMENTS

This book could never have happened without the help of countless individuals in both industry and government throughout the world. While we won't try to name them all, we appreciate the time so many took to provide photographs, drawings and information. A few stand out as extraordinary, and to them a special "thank you": to Terry White, formerly of NASA's Johnson Space Center, for reading the manuscript and for his memory of more than 25 years of American manned space exploration; to Mike Gentry at JSC for his knack for locating photos; and to Nick Johnson at Teledyne Brown Engineering for his generous contribution of drawings and information on the Soviet program. Also to four magazine editors whose curious minds have kept us covering a steady stream of fascinating assignments on space over the years: Tony Reichhardt of *Final Frontier*, John Rhea, formerly of *Space World*, and Kate McMains and Leonard David of *Ad Astra*. And for their supportive enthusiasm, to our agent, Linda Allen; and at Facts On File to James Warren whose vision helped shape the series and Deirdre Mullane who heroically saved the day more than once. Also at Facts On File, our appreciation to Kathy Ishizuka for her patience and organizational powers; Michael Laraque for a fine job of copyediting; Ron Monteleone for creating an outstanding design; and Terri Dieli and Erik Ehn for a difficult production job well done. And our very special thanks for spirited late-night talk and steady encouragement throughout the years to Laurie Wise—scientist, humanitarian and friend. Without you all this book would not be.

INTRODUCTION

*S*pace flights can't be stopped. This isn't the
work of any one man or even a group of men. It
is a historical process which mankind is carrying
out in accordance with the natural laws of
human development.

—Yuri Gagarin

The idea of reaching beyond our world into space was not conceived by
just one man or woman but is the dream of humanity—an undertaking by
thousands who have given their minds, hearts, courage and sometimes their
lives. Space is an airless vacuum, beyond the safety of the cocoon provided
by Earth's atmosphere. It is unforgiving. It is dangerous. And it is demanding.

Like the unsolved puzzle, the unclimbed mountain and the unwritten
book, space calls out to us and challenges us. To engage it requires our finest
thinking, our most brilliant engineering, our most skilled navigation and
our greatest courage; it requires our best.

While we couldn't tell everyone's story, in *Space People From A to Z* we
have included more than 260 of those who have made the greatest contributions—men and women who have flown in space, and many who have
helped put them there.

This book is dedicated to all "space people," those who have risen to the
challenge—the dreamers, the designers, the testers, the pioneers—the
builders who believe that even when you've given your best you can do
even more. It is dedicated to those who have pledged their life's work and
to those who have given their lives to this venture that calls on us to stretch
the boundaries of our universe.

And it is dedicated to the loved ones they left behind.

Acton, Loren

U.S. astronaut
Born: March 7, 1936
Loren Acton, a solar physicist employed by the Lockheed Corporation, flew in space in 1985 as a civilian payload specialist aboard the U.S. Space Shuttle Mission 51-F/Spacelab 2. Acton conducted 13 different experiments during his part of the solar study mission.

Adams, Michael

U.S. test pilot
Born: May 5, 1930
Died: November 15, 1967
X-15 test pilot Michael Adams was killed while making the 191st flight of the U.S.'s most famous experimental plane. He was the only X-15 test flight fatality, with just eight more flights to go before completion of the tests.

Adams, who had flown 49 combat missions in Korea, had joined the Air Force Test Pilot School at Edwards Air Force Base in California in 1962. Originally chosen to participate in the Air Force Manned Orbiting Laboratory program, Adams chose in 1966 to fly the X-15 instead. During his final flight, Adams pushed the X-15 rocket plane to an altitude of 50.4 miles, qualifying him for U.S. Air Force astronaut wings.

Adamson, James C.

U.S. astronaut
Born: March 3, 1946
A colonel in the Army, James Adamson made his first space flight as a mission specialist aboard Shuttle mission STS-28 in August 1989. He and his crew mates traveled aboard the orbiter Columbia, with lift-off on August 8, 1989, carrying military payloads for the Department of Defense as well as several secondary payloads. After 80 orbits they landed successfully at Edwards Air Force Base in California five days later, on August 13.

During a distinguished military career, Adamson earned 23 medals in combat flights in Southeast Asia as well as numerous other awards. A military test pilot, he has logged over 3,000 hours of flight time in over 30 types of helicopters, piston props, turbo props and turbo jet aircraft. He also holds certification as an aerospace engineer and commercial pilot.

Adamson was first employed by NASA at the Johnson Space Center in 1981. In 1985 he became an astronaut and was assigned to fly a Department of Defense mission shortly thereafter when the Challenger accident in 1986 put all Shuttle missions on hold for two and a half years.

Aksenov, Vladimir

Soviet cosmonaut
Born: February 1, 1935
Aksenov has flown two missions as flight engineer aboard the Soviet Soyuz spacecraft. In June 1980 he accompanied Commander Yuri Malyshev on the first manned flight of the Soyuz T model transport (Soyuz T-2), and, after a few docking problems, spent three days aboard the Salyut 6 space station. Prior to his Soyuz T-2 mission, Aksenov was flight engineer aboard the eight-day Soyuz 22 mission (September 1976), which was primarily dedicated to study of the Earth from space.

Aldrin, Buzz

U.S. astronaut
Born: January 20, 1930
"We both landed at the same time," Buzz Aldrin would usually reply when introduced as the "second man to land on the Moon." As lunar module pilot of the most famous flight in space history, Aldrin was the second human to set foot on the Moon, following Apollo 11 Commander Neil Armstrong down the lunar lander's ladder to the Moon's dusty surface only 15 minutes after Armstrong's famous "small step."

"Magnificent desolation," was how Aldrin described the Moon's surface. Somehow it just didn't have the same ring as Armstrong's famous words.

Being the second man to walk the surface of the Moon, though, was a hard act to follow, and that historic mission of July 16–24, 1969, was the restless Buzz Aldrin's last space flight.

Born Edwin E. Aldrin, Jr., in Montclair, New Jersey, he was a West Point graduate and served as a combat pilot in Korea, flying over 60 combat missions before returning to the U.S. to become aide to the dean of faculty at the U.S. Air Force Academy. After three years he moved to Germany and spent the next three years as an F-100 pilot with the 36th Fighter Day Wing at Bitburg. Joining NASA in October 1963, he served as capcom (capsule communicator) for Gemini 5 and

Gemini 10 in August 1965 and July 1966, making his first space flight on Gemini 12, (November 11–15, 1966) the last of the Gemini missions. Spending four days in space in his Gemini mission, Aldrin put in over five hours of EVA (extravehicular activity) in one of the most successful space walks of the Gemini program.

Gemini 12 and Apollo 11 would be Aldrin's only space flights. Resigning from NASA in July 1971 to return to the Air Force, he was appointed commander of the Test Pilot School at Edwards Air Force Base in California. It wasn't an easy time for Buzz Aldrin. A man who often seemed to walk to the sound of a different drummer, he had upset some conservative NASA officials during his tour of duty there by participating in a march after the death of civil rights activist Dr. Martin Luther King. His return to the Air Force was cut short in 1972 when he suffered a nervous breakdown and retired from the service.

The Eagle Has Landed was the name of a popular NASA motion picture detailing the historic flight of Apollo 11. For Buzz Aldrin, who retired from the Air Force in 1972 and returned to civilian life, the rest of the story was best told in his autobiography published in 1973, *Return to Earth* and his 1989 book about the Apollo program, *Men from Earth*.

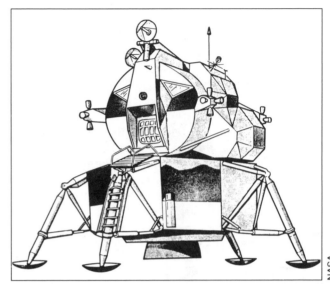

The Apollo lunar module carried six teams of two astronauts to the Moon's surface

Alexandrov, Alexandr

Soviet cosmonaut
Born: February 20, 1943

Fascinated with rockets and space exploration, as a boy "Sasha" Alexandrov kept a scrapbook of clippings on GIRD, the early Soviet rocket study group. Following his military service, he joined Sergei Korolev's spacecraft design bureau, and, after several disappointing attempts, was accepted to the cosmonaut group in December 1978.

During his nearly 150 days in space, he served as flight engineer aboard Soyuz T-9 and participated with Commander Vladimir Lyakhov in one of the most nerve-wracking and eventful spaceflights in Soviet space history. Launched June 27, 1983, Soyuz T-9 docked successfully two days later for a planned four-month stay aboard Salyut 7, which had been linked to an extra module called Cosmos 1443. About a month into their stay they experienced a jolt when a micrometeorite struck a porthole, leaving a visible crater—but no real damage. Trouble really broke out though on September 9 when a fuel pipeline burst during refueling by a Progress cargo vessel. Although the complex was still safe to live in, it was severely damaged, and back on Earth cosmonauts Vladimir Titov and Gennady Strekalov prepared a rescue mission to the space station to take care of repairs. Those plans were quashed, however, by a launchpad fire. Just seconds before ignition Titov and Strekalov became the first to use the escape tower or rocket mounted at the nose of their spacecraft, which lifted

At a press conference prior to his mission, Apollo 11 astronaut Buzz Aldrin describes the lunar module he later pilots to the Moon's surface

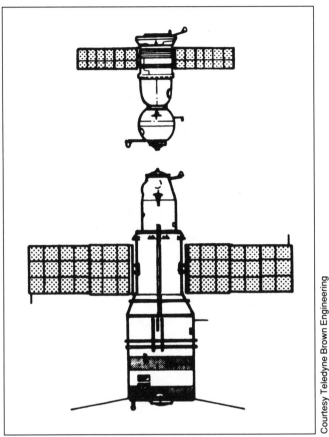

Salyut 7 and approaching Soyuz spacecraft

Courtesy Teledyne Brown Engineering

Soyuz T-10-1 up and away before the booster below exploded. Free from danger, they parachuted to safety. The mission never lifted off, of course, and damage to the launchpad prevented any further rescue plans for the moment.

Virtually stranded in a cold, damp space station, Alexandrov and Lyakhov made two space walks on November 1 and 3 without the usual training and completed the repairs themselves. They returned safely to Earth on November 23.

Alexandrov also stepped in five years later to relieve Alexander Laveikin, who fell ill while going for an endurance record aboard the Mir space station with Yuri Romanenko in 1987. Arriving in July aboard the Soyuz TM-3 with Muhammed Faris and Alexander Viktorenko, Alexandrov stayed on with Romanenko, returning to Earth December 21, 1987.

Alexandrov, Alexandr

Bulgarian cosmonaut
Born: December 1, 1951
The second Bulgarian to fly in space, Alexandr Alexandrov was originally primed as backup for the Soyuz 33 mission flown by his compatriot Georgy Ivanov in April 1979. Nine years later, however, Alexandrov did get his chance, flying with Anatoliy Solovyov and Viktor Savinykh on the Soyuz TM-5 mission to Mir space station in June 1988.

Allen, Joseph

U.S. scientist/astronaut
Born: June 27, 1937
A mission specialist aboard U.S. Space Shuttle mission 51-A (November 8–16, 1984) and mission STS-5 (November 11–16, 1982), Allen has some 11 hours of EVA (extravehicular activity) time to his credit. Along with fellow astronaut Dale Gardner, he participated in the first salvage mission in space history on mission 51-A when in the course of two space walks he and Gardner retrieved two troubled satellites.

During the first retrieval, of the Palapa B-2, the pair of space workers discovered that the system devised to grapple the huge satellite with the Remote Manipulator Arm wouldn't work. They ended up having to bully Palapa into the cargo bay themselves, with Allen holding it (unwieldy though weightless) over his head for one entire orbit around the Earth while Gardner devised a method to lock it in place.

Allen, who holds a doctorate in physics, left NASA in 1985 to join Space Industries, Inc.

Anders, William

U.S. astronaut
Born: October 17, 1933
Aboard Apollo 8 (December 21–27, 1968) Bill Anders was one of the first three men to orbit the Moon. Anders, along with Frank Borman and James Lovell, began their historic orbit on Christmas Eve 1968 after escaping from Earth orbit via NASA's Apollo workhorse, the powerful Saturn 5 rocket. Circling the Moon 10 times, the crew of Apollo 8 were the first humans ever to see its far side with their own eyes. After his historic flight, Anders became executive secretary for the National Aeronautics and Space Council in 1969 and remained with the council until 1973, when he was appointed to the Atomic Energy Commission. Later serving as first chairman of the Nuclear Regulatory Commission in 1975, he left in 1976 to become U.S. ambassador to Norway. He left government service in 1977 to enter private industry. Apollo 8 was Anders' only space flight.

That's one small step for a man, one giant leap for mankind.
　　—Neil Armstrong, as he stepped on the Moon

Armstrong, Neil

U.S. astronaut
Born: August 5, 1930

The man who took "a giant step for mankind" by becoming the first human being to step on the Moon, Neil Armstrong was born on a farm outside Wapakoneta, Ohio. Always fascinated by flying, he spent his youth building model airplanes and received his student pilot's license on his 16th birthday. He attended Purdue University on a U.S. Navy scholarship in 1947, but left a year and a half later when he was called to active duty. Attending flight school in Pensacola, Florida, he became a fighter pilot and was later assigned to Fighter Squadron 51 in Korea. It was a harrowing experience for the young pilot. Flying 78 missions during the Korean War, he was shot down twice. His love of the skies still remained, though, and after his military

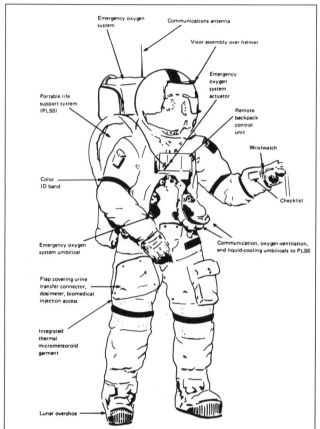

The space suit used by Apollo astronauts during EVAs on the Moon's surface

U.S. astronaut Neil Armstrong, the first human being to walk on the Moon

service he returned to Purdue in 1952 where he received a B.S. in aeronautical engineering in 1955.

He was on a path that would lead him to fame when he went to work for the National Advisory Committee on Aeronautics (NACA), which would later become the National Aeronautics and Space Administration (NASA). Assigned to Edwards Air Force Base deep in the Mojave Desert, Armstrong became a test pilot, flying such advanced aircraft as the X-15 rocket plane at heights of over 200,000 feet and speeds of more than 4,000 miles per hour.

All told, Armstrong spent over 1,100 hours in the air. Space was beginning to beckon top test pilots and Armstrong became one of the first two civilian astronauts chosen for America's manned space program. As command pilot of Gemini 8 (March 1966), he performed the first successful docking of two vehicles in space.

The modest and very private Armstrong then went on to make history when at 4:18 p.m. Eastern daylight time, June 20, 1969, the Apollo 11 landing module descended on the Moon's dusty surface.

"That's one small step for a man, one giant leap for mankind," were Armstrong's first words upon setting foot on the Moon's barren face.

Planting the American flag, Armstrong and fellow astronaut Buzz Aldrin remained on the moon for 21 hours and 37 minutes, returning to Earth and splashdown at sea on July 24, 1969. The mission had taken eight days, and for many it was the most important eight days in the history of human exploration.

Resigning from NASA in August 1971 to become a professor of aerospace engineering at the University of Cincinnati, Armstrong later worked in private industry. A quiet man who likes his privacy, Armstrong was once again in the public eye in 1984 when he participated in the National Commission on Space, whose job it was to develop long-term goals for the space program. When the U.S. Space Shuttle Challenger exploded during launch on January 28, 1986, Armstrong was named vice-chairman of the investigating committee. He has since returned to private life.

Artyukhin, Yuri

Soviet cosmonaut
Born: July 22, 1940
The son of a Soviet air force bombardier who was killed in action, Artyukhin was forced to drop out of air force flight school because of health problems. Staying in the service he enrolled in technical school and became an expert in military communications systems. After joining the cosmonaut group in 1963, his talents were put to use as a member of the first successful Soviet space station crew aboard Salyut 3, in 1974. Although Artyukhin and fellow cosmonaut Pavel Popovich were engaged in medical and communications experiments during their two-week stay, most Western observers believe that the mission was the first of the "military" Salyut missions, operating in low Earth orbit and communicating to and from Earth in code.

Atkov, Oleg

Soviet cosmonaut
Born: May 9, 1949
Oleg Atkov, a medical doctor, spent more than 237 days in space as a member of the Soyuz T-10 mission to the Soviet space station Salyut 7 (February–October, 1984). Atkov, who had designed a portable ultrasound cardiograph for use on Soviet space flights, spent his time aboard Salyut studying the effects of space on himself and fellow crew members Leonid Kizim and Vladimir Solovyov.

B

Bagian, James P.

U.S. astronaut
Born: February 22, 1952
A physician, James Bagian made his first space flight of 119 hours as mission specialist aboard the orbiter Discovery, Shuttle mission STS-29. After lift-off on March 13, 1989, the five-member crew deployed a Tracking and Data Relay Satellite (TDRS) and performed several experiments in space, including a "heat pipe" experiment to test technology that might be used on the Space Station Freedom, two student experiments, a protein crystal growth experiment, and a chromosome and plant cell division experiment. The crew also took more than 3,000 photographs of the Earth using several types of cameras and a movie camera. The mission was successfully completed after 80 orbits, with Discovery landing at Edwards Air Force Base on March 18.

Bagian's extensive background as a flight surgeon and in aerospace medicine gives him special insights into the effects of microgravity on humans and other living organisms. He is slated to fly again aboard STS-40, a dedicated space and life sciences mission scheduled for June 1990.

Baker, Ellen S.

U.S. astronaut
Born: April 27, 1953
Baker, a physician, made her first space flight in October 1989 aboard the orbiter Discovery, on Mission STS-34. Launched on October 17, with Donald Williams, Michael McCulley, Shannon Lucid and Franklin Chang-Díaz, Baker helped deploy the Galileo spacecraft, a state-of-the-art planetary probe to Jupiter and its moons. They landed successfully at Edwards Air Force Base five days later on October 23.

An astronaut qualified for assignment since 1985, Baker is a graduate with honors from the Air Force Aerospace Medicine Primary Course at Brooks Air Force Base in San Antonio, Texas. Before she was selected as an astronaut candidate she served as a physician in the Flight Medicine Clinic at Johnson Space Center.

Bartoe, John-David

U.S. astronaut
Born: November 17, 1944

As a payload specialist aboard U.S. Space Shuttle mission 51-F (July 29–August 6, 1985), Bartoe spent eight days operating a solar ultraviolet telescope of his own design as well as a number of other astronomical experiments. A researcher at the U.S. Naval Research Laboratory in Washington, D.C., Bartoe holds a Ph.D. from Georgetown University.

Baudry, Patrick

French "spationaut"
Born: March 6, 1946

As a French "spationaut," a name chosen by the French to signify that their space flyers are aligned neither with the United States (astronauts) nor with the Soviet Union (cosmonauts), Baudry served as a payload specialist on U.S. Space Shuttle mission 51-G (June 17–24, 1985). Among his fellow crew members was the first Arab to fly aboard a U.S. shuttle, Sultan al-Saud.

Baudry also served as backup for fellow spationaut Jean-Loup Chrétien for the Soviet Soyuz T-6 flight to the Salyut 7 space station in 1982.

Bean, Alan

U.S. astronaut
Born: March 15, 1932

Presently a professional artist whose space paintings have been displayed in the National Air and Space Museum, Alan Bean lives in Houston, Texas. His paintings, like those of Russian cosmonaut-artist Alexei Leonov, are enhanced not only by his creative imagination but by his actual space experiences; he was the fourth human to walk on the Moon.

Bean's moonwalk on November 18, 1969, came after he and Commander Charles Conrad landed the lunar module of Apollo 12 on the surface of our nearest space neighbor. It was a near pin-point landing, only about 600 feet away from the U.S. Surveyor 3, which had landed 31 months before. Curiously, among the parts of Surveyor returned to Earth by Bean and Conrad, scientists found a colony of bacteria in the foam insulation of Surveyor's TV camera surviving after over 2½ years. It could be said Bean and Conrad "encountered" life on the Moon.

In one of the most successful of the Apollo missions, Bean and Conrad spent over 30 hours walking

Astronaut Alan Bean using a battery-powered shaver aboard Skylab, where he spent 59½ days in Earth orbit with fellow astronauts Owen Garriott and Jack Lousma from July to September 1973

the Moon's dusty surface before returning to Earth on November 24, 1969.

Ironically, in light of Bean's later ability to convey the colors and mystery of space, the only real mishap of Apollo 12 occurred when he accidentally pointed a color television camera at the Sun, burning it out and preventing color pictures from being transmitted to viewers on Earth.

Bean commanded his second and last flight aboard Skylab 3, the second of three manned missions on America's first space station. With fellow astronauts Owen Garriott and Jack Lousma, Bean spent over 59 days, from July 28 until September 25, 1973, conducting experiments and making observations of the Earth and Sun.

Although he was in line to command the first of the Shuttle/Spacelab missions, Bean decided to work full time as an artist and resigned from NASA on June 26, 1981.

Beggs, James M.

NASA administrator
Born: January 9, 1926

Formerly executive vice president and a director of General Dynamics Corporation in St. Louis, James M. Beggs became head of NASA on July 10, 1981, and served in that capacity until May 1986. Prior to that he had served with NASA as an associate administrator in the Office of Advanced Research and

Technology from 1968 to 1969 and was under secretary of transportation from 1969 to 1973.

Belyayev, Pavel

Soviet cosmonaut
Born: June 26, 1925
Died: January 10, 1970

A military pilot before becoming a part of the Soviet cosmonaut team, Pavel Belyayev was commander aboard Voskhod 2 when fellow cosmonaut Alexei Leonov made the world's first space walk (March 18, 1965). Upon its return the spacecraft ran into trouble and Belyayev was forced to take over the controls and make a manual reentry. Although the crew landed safely, they were far off course and after the rigors of their space flight were forced to endure another cold two days waiting in the wilderness until a rescue team arrived to help them. Belyayev died from peritonitis following an operation for stomach ulcers in 1970.

Beregovoy, Georgy

Soviet cosmonaut
Born: April 15, 1921

The first Soviet test pilot to fly in space, Georgy Beregovoy, at age 47 (making him also the oldest cosmonaut at that time), flew aboard Soyuz 3 (October 1968). After his flight, Beregovoy, who had also flown over 180 combat missions against the Nazis in World War II, was appointed director of the Gagarin Cosmonaut Training Center.

Berezovoy, Anatoly

Soviet cosmonaut
Born: April 11, 1942

Commanding the first flight to the soviet space station Salyut 7 on the seven-month Soyuz T-5 mission (May–December 1982), Berezovoy and engineer Valentin Lebedev, played host to visiting cosmonauts from Soyuz T-6 and T-7 in June and August of that year. Among the two groups were French "spationaut" Jean-Loup Chrétien and the second Soviet woman in space, Svetlana Savitskaya.

Ironically, after seven months in space Berezovoy and Lebedev found their first night back on Earth unexpectedly dangerous and uncomfortable when their spacecraft returned in the middle of a cold and fog-shrouded night. The craft apparently tumbled down a hillside, making rescue difficult. One helicopter crashed in the attempt, and a second had to be "talked down" by them before they could be retrieved and given shelter before returning to the launch complex the next morning.

Blaha, John

U.S. astronaut
Born: August 26, 1942

Originally assigned to pilot his first space flight in June 1986, following the Challenger tragedy in January 1986 John Blaha helped improve the safety of the Space Shuttle by working on modifications to its hardware. He also contributed to new plans for emergency abort procedures. His first opportunity to fly in space came in March 1989 when he piloted STS-29 (March 13–18), an eventful mission during which the crew took more than 3,000 photographs and movies of the Earth, deployed a TDRS (Tracking and Data Relay System) satellite and performed numerous experiments. He also piloted STS-33, a Department of Defense mission flown in November 1989.

Bluford, Guion

U.S. astronaut
Born: November 22, 1942

As a mission specialist aboard the U.S. Space Shuttle mission STS-8 (August 30–September 5, 1983) Guion Bluford was the first black American to go into space.

Mission specialist Guion Bluford using the exercise treadmill aboard the U.S. Space Shuttle

ORBITER ACCOMMODATIONS
Seats, restraints, and mobility aids
Egress systems
Flight data file
Sighting aids
Photographic equipment
Window shades and filters
Stowage areas
Food systems and equipment
Sleeping accommodations
Crew hygiene systems and accommodations
Housekeeping equipment
Airlock

CREW EQUIPMENT
Survival equipment
Medical kits
Radiation instrumentation
Operational bioinstrumentation
Crew clothing
Space suit assembly

NASA

Crew quarters aboard the U.S. Space Shuttle are located on the flight deck and mid deck in the nose of the Orbiter. The crew can access the depressurized cargo bay (where the Spacelab module is located during a Spacelab mission) through the round airlock hatch on the mid deck

He made a second flight aboard Mission 61-A/Spacelab D1 (October 30–November 6, 1985) as part of an eight-astronaut team on a mission directed by the Federal German Aerospace Research Establishment. Bluford holds a Ph.D. in aerospace engineering.

Bobko, Karol

U.S. astronaut
Born: December 23, 1937
As an Air Force officer assigned to the ill-fated Manned Orbiting Laboratory in 1966, Karol Bobko survived the disappointment of the abrupt cancellation of that program and flew instead aboard three different U.S. Space Shuttle orbiters. Transferring to NASA in 1969 as an astronaut, Bobko made his first flight in April 1983 as pilot of the maiden voyage of the Shuttle Challenger. He commanded mission 51-D aboard the orbiter Discovery (April 12–19, 1985) and the maiden voyage of Atlantis, mission 51-J (October 3–7) that same year.

Bolden, Charles

U.S. astronaut
Born: August 19, 1946
As pilot of U.S. Space Shuttle mission 61-C (January 12–18, 1986), Charles Bolden had the distinction of waiting through seven different launch delays before lift-off as well as of carrying America's second space-bound politician, Florida congressman Bill Nelson, aboard. During the six-day flight the crew released the RCA Satcom Ku-1 satellite.

Shuttle mission 61-C was the last successful U.S. space mission before the tragic mission 51-L Challenger disaster, which carried seven astronauts to their deaths on January 28, 1986.

Bondarenko, Valentin

Soviet cosmonaut
Born: 1936
Died: March 23, 1961
The first space traveler (astronaut or cosmonaut) to die in training, Valentin Bondarenko was killed in a pressure-chamber fire on March 23, 1961, only three weeks before the historic flight of the first Soviet cosmonaut, Yuri Gagarin. The fire that killed Bondarenko is believed to have started when a cotton swab dipped in alcohol was accidentally tossed onto a hot plate inside the oxygen-rich pressure chamber. The youngest of the original group of Soviet cosmonauts, Bondarenko was a senior lieutenant in the Soviet air force.

Bonestell, Chesley

U.S. space artist
Born: 1888
Died: 1986
The recipient of a special award from the British Interplanetary Society, Chesley Bonestell was the world's best-known space artist, inspiring a generation of space enthusiasts, writers and other artists. Although he trained to be an architect, he never completed his studies and spent his early years working in various architectural offices in San Francisco, California. He later worked as an artist, doing background paintings and mats for such motion pictures as *Citizen Kane* (1941), *Destination Moon* (1950), *When Worlds Collide* (1951) and *War of the Worlds* (1953). From the early 1940s until the 1970s he specialized in works depicting the facts and wonders of space, producing over 10 books, including his most famous, *The Conquest of Space* (1949), with a text by rocket pioneer Willy Ley. A 10 x 40 foot mural he originally did for the Boston Museum of Science in

1950 and 1951 was transferred to the Smithsonian Institution's National Air and Space Museum in 1976.

Borman, Frank

U.S. astronaut
Born: March 14, 1928
As commander of Apollo 8 (December 21–27, 1968), Frank Borman, along with fellow astronauts James Lovell and William Anders, made 10 orbits of the Moon. It was on this mission that Borman earned the dubious distinction of becoming the first astronaut to vomit in space (but certainly not the first to experience space sickness). Borman also found himself involved in an unusual controversy upon his return home. At NASA's request, the three Apollo 8 crewmen had read passages from the Bible on a live Christmas Eve broadcast from lunar orbit. The act drew some angry protest and even a threatened legal suit to "stop the astronauts from broadcasting religious propaganda from space."

Borman's only previous space flight had been aboard Gemini 7 (December 4–18, 1965), when he and copilot James Lovell joined up with Gemini 6-A and

Astronaut Frank Borman, commander of the Apollo 8 mission to the Moon, takes part in a training exercise aboard the Apollo Mission Simulator in Houston, Texas

its crew of Wally Schirra and James Stafford for NASA's first space rendezvous. On that flight Borman and Lovell also went on to set a new space endurance record of 14 days. Borman retired from NASA in 1970 to join Eastern Airlines.

Brand, Vance

U.S. astronaut
Born: May 9, 1931
Vance Brand came close to becoming a space casualty when he and fellow astronauts Deke Slayton and Thomas Stafford returned to Earth after their historic Apollo-Soyuz mission (July 15–24, 1975). The mission, a joint U.S. and Soviet rendezvous and docking, had gone without a hitch. Televised pictures had been sent to viewers in both countries of a historic handshake in space, and the astronauts and cosmonauts exchanged visits to each other's spacecraft, performed a few joint experiments, and shared meals before separating to return to Earth. It was upon Apollo's return that tragedy nearly struck. A confusion in procedure after entering the Earth's atmosphere resulted in an open valve on the Apollo spacecraft, permitting deadly nitrogen tetroxide from a thruster to enter the vehicle. During splashdown all three men were fighting to remain conscious, but Brand, knocked about the wave-pounded spacecraft, passed out; only quick action by Slayton and Stafford in getting an oxygen mask on him saved his life. Although all three astronauts suffered temporary lung damage, no permanent harm had been inflicted, and viewers watching the historic splashdown weren't even aware of the close call faced by the crew on board the bobbing spacecraft.

Following Apollo-Soyuz, Brand went to work on the development of the U.S. Space Shuttle and to command the first shuttle operational mission, STS-5 (November 11–16, 1982), as well as mission 41–B (February 3–11, 1984).

Brandenstein, Daniel

U.S. astronaut
Born: January 17, 1943
Prior to serving with NASA, Daniel Brandenstein had been a U.S. Navy Test Pilot and instructor. His years of training paid off when he piloted the STS-8 Challenger mission in 1983, the first U.S. Space Shuttle to launch and land at night. In June 1985, Captain Brandenstein also commanded mission 51-G, which carried aboard Saudi prince Sultan al-Saud.

Brandenstein is now chief of the Mission Support Branch in the Astronaut Office at Johnson Space Center.

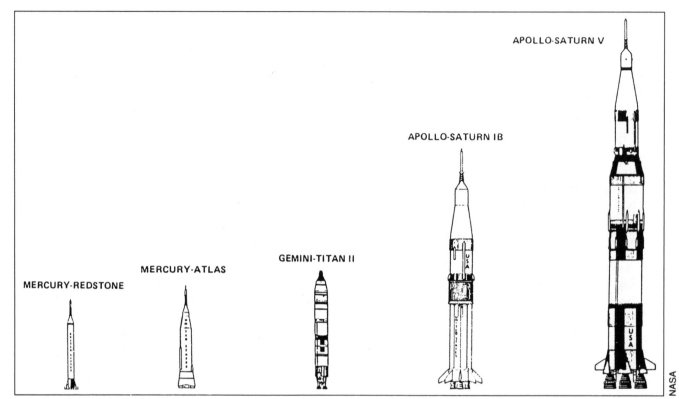

APOLLO-SATURN V

APOLLO-SATURN IB

GEMINI-TITAN II

MERCURY-ATLAS

MERCURY-REDSTONE

NASA

From Mercury to Apollo, development of the rockets that took the first American astronauts into space was in large measure due to the vision and skill of Wernher von Braun

Braun, Wernher von

German-American rocket engineer
Born: March 23, 1912
Died: June 16, 1977

The controversial genius behind the early days of the United States' space program, Wernher von Braun was responsible for America's first space success, the satellite Explorer 1, launched January 31, 1958.

Born in Germany and educated in Switzerland and Berlin, he became interested in rocketry and the idea of space travel after reading a book by Hermann Oberth while still a teen. Joining the German Rocket Society in 1930, he aided in the firing of over 80 rockets. When the society disbanded in 1932, some members began working on rocketry for the German army while others dropped out of what was clearly becoming a military, not a space project. Undeterred by politics, though, von Braun stayed on to pursue his all-consuming interest in rockets. By the time Hitler assumed full power in 1933 von Braun had become one of Germany's most influential rocket pioneers. Working under the command of Walter Dornberger at Peenemünde when World War II broke out, von Braun and his fellow engineers and scientists began full-scale development of rockets for military purposes.

Although still primarily concerned with the idea of rockets for space flight, the von Braun group became the pioneers of deadly guided missiles as well. Von Braun joined the Nazi party in 1940 and by 1942 had developed a weapon capable of carrying its own fuel and oxygen and able to reach a height of 60 miles.

Von Braun's missile, called the V-2 and built with slave labor, was developed too late to rescue the German army from defeat, but in its short history the V-2 terrorized the Allies. Over 4,300 such missiles were fired; more than 1,200 hit London, England, killing more than 2,500 people and seriously injuring thousands of others. United States intelligence officers after the war later calculated that more than 3,000 people used as slaves by the Nazis to build the missiles may have died of mistreatment or in accidents.

Fleeing from advancing Russian troops near the end of the war, von Braun and his team surrendered to the American Army after deciding that they would be given better treatment by the United States than by Russia, whose countryside the Nazis had ravaged. It was a politically astute move. Von Braun and his group were secretly smuggled into the United States under the government program known as Operation

Wernher von Braun, the German-American rocket pioneer whose vision galvanized the U.S. space program

Paperclip and began working openly and with few restrictions on the fledgling American rocket program.

As vocal an advocate in the United States for space exploration and colonization as he had been in Germany in his early days, von Braun went on to become a driving force behind the Saturn 5 rocket that later took the first humans to the Moon, as well as a popular author and speaker in defense of America's space program.

Bridges, Roy

U.S. astronaut
Born: July 19, 1943
Pilot of U.S. Space Shuttle mission 51-F (July 29–August 6, 1985), an eight-day Spacelab 2 mission concerned primarily with astronomical research. The mission started out with several nerve-wracking setbacks, including a launchpad abort (with no lift-off) on July 12, and, after launch on July 29, a main-engine failure that initially left the orbiter in too low an orbit. Then the Instrument Pointing System (costing $60 million), designed to point the mission's telescopes, broke down. Through maneuvering and cooperation between crew and ground control, however, the experiments were salvaged, uncovering new informa-

tion about the upper atmosphere, the Sun and the rest of the universe.

A colonel in the Air Force, Bridges was also scheduled to pilot Shuttle mission 61-F in May 1986, which was to send NASA's Galileo mission on its way to explore Jupiter. Bridges returned to Air Force duty instead, however, after the Challenger disaster put the U.S. space program on hold in January 1986.

Brown, Mark

U.S. astronaut
Born: November 18, 1951
On his first space flight Mark Brown served as a mission specialist aboard the orbiter Atlantis on U.S. Shuttle mission STS-28 (August 8–13, 1989). Carrying Department of Defense payloads and several secondary payloads, the five-member crew made 80 orbits of the Earth in five days, landing on a dry lakebed at Edwards Air Force Base in California.

Following the Challenger accident in 1986 Brown served as a member of the team that redesigned the solid rocket booster that had played a critical part in causing that disaster. He is a colonel in the U.S. Air Force and holds an M.S. in astronautical engineering.

Buchli, James

U.S. astronaut
Born: June 20, 1945
Serving as a mission specialist on three U.S. Space Shuttle flights, Buchli assisted in a classified Department of Defense payload on mission 51-C, January 1985, flew with the German Spacelab mission, 61-A, in October–November that same year, and helped take photographs of Earth aboard STS-29 in March 1989.

In a televised interview from space, Buchli told "Today" show watchers on NBC-TV about the dramatic view of damage to Earth's environment the crew had filmed from orbit. Using a 70 mm movie camera, the STS-29 crew filmed the Earth to enable people, Buchli said, to see "just how much we are dumping into the atmosphere and perhaps get a feel for how that might affect us in future generations." With the high-powered lens the crew was able to capture images of our scarred planet— including pollution in the ocean, floods in Africa, burned patches of the Florida Everglades and vast areas of damage to the tropical rain forest in South America.

A graduate of Annapolis, Buchli is a colonel in the U.S. Marine Corps. During his three Shuttle missions he has logged 15 days in space.

Bykovsky, Valery
Soviet cosmonaut
Born: August 2, 1934
Valery Bykovsky made space history in 1963, when in June of that year he spent nearly five days alone in the Vostok 5 spacecraft, the longest solo space flight up to that date. Later Bykovsky commanded Soyuz 22 (1976) and Soyuz 31 (1978), both scientific missions.

C

Carpenter, Scott
U.S. astronaut
Born: May 1, 1925
"Spectacular, like a very brilliant rainbow," was how Scott Carpenter described his first sunset viewed from Earth orbit aboard Mercury 7 (May 24, 1962). The second American astronaut to orbit the Earth, Carpenter circled three times but used up too much fuel and fell behind schedule. As a result he was forced to reenter the Earth's atmosphere under manual control and splashed down 250 miles from his recovery ship. He was safely retrieved 40 minutes after splashdown, but not before some television newscasters announced to their nervous viewers that America might have "lost an astronaut."

Critical of Carpenter's performance during the flight, some NASA officials held him responsible for the anxious moments surrounding his recovery. Mercury 7 was his only space flight. In 1965, taking a leave of absence from NASA, he participated in the Navy's Sealab 2 experiment, spending 30 days living and working in another alien environment, the challenging depths of the ocean floor. After retiring from NASA he continued with the Sealab experiments and served as assistant for aquanaut operations for Sealab 3. In 1969 he retired from the Navy with the rank of commander and became an engineering consultant and wasp breeder.

Carr, Gerald
U.S. astronaut
Born: August 22, 1932
As commander of the longest U.S. manned space flight, Skylab 4 (November 16, 1973–February 8, 1974), Gerald Carr was a participant, along with fellow astronauts Edward Gibson and William Pogue, in the first and only "strike" in spaceflight history. Burdened by an impossibly heavy work schedule placed on them by NASA ground controllers who were still "up" from the successful Skylab 3 mission, Carr, Gibson and Pogue were at first content merely to grumble about their difficulties. They complained about everything. Their work schedule was too heavy. The food was bad. The station design was bad. The toilet didn't work properly and the interior of the space station was the wrong color. When the grumbling didn't help solve their real problem—their unrealistic schedule—they decided to sit things out for a day or so. After an embarrassed and nervous ground control set up a hasty "bull-session" between the crew and ground staff, work resumed at a normal, less demanding pace. Skylab 4 eventually went on to become one of the most successful of all Skylab missions.

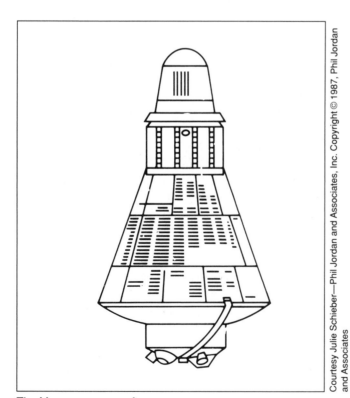

The Mercury spacecraft

Courtesy Julie Schieber—Phil Jordan and Associates, Inc. Copyright © 1987, Phil Jordan and Associates

Skylab 4 was Carr's only space flight. After the mission he was appointed head of the astronaut office Shuttle design support group. Retiring from the Marine Corps in 1975 and from NASA in 1977, he entered private industry as a consultant and has contributed design ideas to the U.S. International Space Station Freedom.

Carter, Manley

U.S. astronaut
Born: August 15, 1947
A captain in the U.S. Navy, "Sonny" Carter made his first space flight aboard the orbiter Discovery on mission STS-33 (November 22–27, 1989), a dedicated Department of Defense flight. Carter graduated from medical school in June 1973, served tours in the U.S. Navy as flight surgeon and as a fighter pilot, and graduated from U.S. Naval Test Pilot School in 1974. In 1984 he was selected by NASA; he qualified for assignment in 1985 and served as extravehicular activity (EVA) representative for the Mission Development Branch of the Astronaut Office.

Cenker, Robert

U.S. astronaut
Born: November 5, 1948
Bob Cenker, an RCA satellite engineer, served as civilian payload specialist aboard U.S. Space Shuttle mission 61-C. Cenker's primary responsibility was to oversee the deployment of RCA's Satcom Ku-1 satellite. A specialist in aerospace and electrical engineering, he has worked for RCA since 1972.

Cernan, Eugene

U.S. astronaut
Born: March 14, 1934
Neil Armstrong had been the first of the Apollo astronauts to walk on the Moon. Eugene Cernan was the last. Along with fellow crewman geologist Harrison Schmitt, Cernan spent more than 22 hours on the Moon, while the third member of the Apollo 17 (December 7–19, 1972) crew, Ronald Evans, orbited overhead.

Unfortunately humankind's last official words from the Moon lacked some of the punch of the first. A few of his associates at Houston suggested he might stand on the porch of the LM, face the camera mounted on the rover and, using Porky Pig's Loony Tunes cartoon sign-off exclaim, "A-bee, a-bee, that's all folks!" However, Cernan said, "As we leave the Moon at Taurus-Littrow, we leave as we came and,

God willing, as we shall return, with peace and hope for all mankind. God bless the crew of Apollo 17."

In his two previous space flights, Cernan had been pilot of Gemini 9-A (June 3–6, 1966) and lunar module pilot of Apollo 10 (May 18–26, 1969), which had flown to within 10 miles of the Moon in a test flight.

A former Navy pilot, Cernan resigned from NASA to enter private industry.

We've got a bad fire—let's get out...We're burning up!
—Roger Chaffee, aboard Apollo 1, in his last
recorded words

Chaffee, Roger

U.S. astronaut
Born: February 15, 1935
Died: January 27, 1967
America's first space tragedy took place on January 27, 1967, when Roger Chaffee, Edward White and Gus Grissom were killed in a flash fire aboard the Apollo 1 spacecraft while training for the first manned Apollo flight. The mission would have been Roger Chaffee's first space flight.

Chaffee, who received a B.S. in aeronautical engineering from Purdue University, was an experienced pilot who had logged nearly 2,300 hours of flying time. As a member of the Heavy Photographic Squadron 62, he had flown photo-reconnaissance missions over Cuba during the Cuban Missile Crisis of 1962.

Chang-Díaz, Franklin

U.S. astronaut
Born: April 5, 1950
Chang-Díaz, the first Hispanic-American astronaut (though not the first Hispanic in space), served aboard U.S. Space Shuttle mission 61-C and again aboard STS-34. Mission 61-C, launched January 12, 1986 after numerous delays, failed in its attempt to observe Halley's Comet but successfully deployed an RCA communications satellite. It was the last Shuttle mission prior to the Challenger accident on January 28 in which all seven crew members were lost.

Just over a year after Shuttle flights resumed in 1988, Chang-Díaz was to fly in space once again, aboard for the historic release of the Galileo spacecraft to Jupiter and its moons. Once again, however, the Shuttle launch slated for October 1989 was delayed. Since the Challenger accident, some environmentalists had become concerned about possible dangers

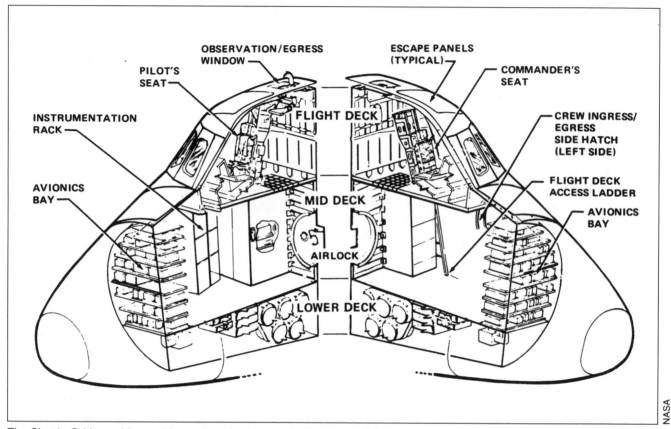

The Shuttle Orbiter cabin provides a place for the crew to live and work in space, with flight operations on the upper flight deck and most experiments (other than EVAs or Spacelab work) done on the mid deck. The airlock on the mid deck allows astronauts to exit during flight for EVAs

in the event of a similar explosion with the nuclear-powered Galileo spacecraft aboard, and several groups sued to stop the Shuttle lift-off. Declared safe by the courts, though, once again the orbiter Atlantis readied for launch, only to be stalled again by computer problems. Finally, Atlantis lifted off without a hitch on October 17, and six and a half hours later the crew successfully sent Galileo on its 2.4-billion-mile, six-year journey. They then turned their attention to studies of the damaged ozone layer of Earth's atmosphere. STS-34 landed at Edwards Air Force Base on October 23.

As a youngster in Costa Rica, Franklin Ramón Chang-Díaz was inspired by Sputnik and wrote to Wernher von Braun asking how to become an astronaut, who advised him to study science. At the age of 17, Chang-Díaz arrived in Hartford, Connecticut, to live with relatives. Ten years later he earned a Ph.D. in applied plasma physics from the Massachusetts Institute of Technology. In 1980 he was selected by NASA to become an astronaut. Six years later he fulfilled his dream, but his October 1989 flight was an even greater triumph with its long-awaited

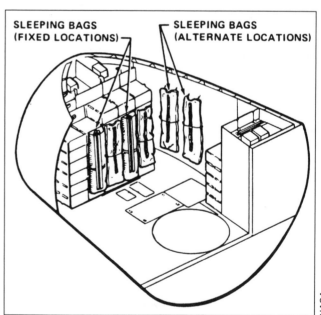

Sleeping bags are located in two areas on the Shuttle Orbiter mid deck. Since there is no "up" or "down" in space, astronauts sleep as comfortably floating against the wall as they would in any other position

send-off of the sophisticated Galileo spacecraft, a mission that had been in the making for more than 20 years.

Chrétien, Jean-Loup

French "spationaut"
Born: August 20, 1938

Serving as a researcher aboard the Soviet Soyuz T-6 (June-July 1982), French spationaut Jean-Loup Chrétien was the first Western participant in the Soviet space program. Spending eight days in space, including seven aboard the space station Salyut 7, Chrétien supervised the operation of a specially built heart monitoring system for use in space health studies.

Chrétien made his second space flight aboard Soyuz TM-7, visiting Mir space station from November 26–December 21, 1988. He was accompanied by Soviet cosmonauts Alexandr Volkov and Sergei Krikalov. During his stay aboard Mir, Chrétien became the first West European to perform a space walk, spending over six hours outside the space station with Volkov, repairing and testing an erectable French-made lattice structure designed to be sprung open by remote control. He returned to Earth aboard Soyuz TM-6 with long-duration cosmonauts Vladimir Titov and Musa Manarov, who were completing a 366-day stay in space.

Chrétien was also backup for French spationaut Patrick Baudry aboard U.S. Shuttle mission 51-G, flown in May 1985, and trained with him in Houston.

When a distinguished but elderly scientist states that something is possible, he is almost certainly right. When he states that something is impossible, he is very probably wrong.
—Arthur C. Clarke

Clarke, Arthur C.

British author
Born: December 16, 1917

A graduate of King's College, London, with honors in physics and mathematics, Arthur C. Clarke is a past chairman of the British Interplanetary Society and a member of the Academy of Astronautics and the Royal Astronomical Society. The author of over 50 books, his work has been translated in more than 30 languages and he has been the recipient of prizes in both the science and science-fiction fields. Best known to the general public for his science-fiction writing, including the popular novel and later hit motion picture *2001*, his now-famous 1945 technical

paper describing geostationary orbits helped form the basis of today's communications satellite systems. Today, in a way he first imagined, space above the equator at 23,000 miles is jammed with communications satellites in geostationary, or geosynchronous, orbit. That is, they seem to hover in one spot because they are traveling at that location at exactly the same speed as the Earth's rotation.

Clarke has also earned the love of every science student and science-fiction buff with his famous words of caution: "When a distinguished but elderly scientist states that something is possible, he is almost certainly right. When he states that something is impossible he is very probably wrong."

Clarke joined newscaster Walter Cronkite as part of televised coverage of many of the U.S. Apollo missions, sharing his insights for the benefit of television viewers of the historic Moon flights.

The early astronauts were the explorers. We are the homesteaders.
—Mary Cleave

Cleave, Mary

U.S. astronaut
Born: February 5, 1947

Cleave, who holds B.S. and M.S. degrees in microbial ecology and a Ph.D. in civil and environmental engineering, qualified as a mission specialist for U.S. Space Shuttle flights in 1981. In November-December 1985 she operated the Shuttle's remote manipulator

Mistakes in space are costly. So astronauts who will be using the Remote Manipulator Arm to perform tasks aboard the Shuttle train on the ground, guiding a working model of the giant arm

arm, testing space construction techniques, on mission 61-B (November 26-December 3).

With her second flight, Cleave was the first woman to fly aboard the Shuttle following the Challenger accident in 1986. She and the rest of the crew aboard STS-30 (May 4-8, 1989) were responsible for sending the planetary spacecraft Magellan on its way to Venus. With completion of this flight, Cleave has logged 262 hours in space.

Cleaver, A.V.

British engineer
Born: ?
Died: 1977
A leading space activist, Cleaver was a member of the British Interplanetary Society and served as chairman in the 1950s. The author of many papers on space technology, exploration and development, Cleaver also worked as chief engineer and manager of the Rocket Department of Rolls-Royce, Ltd, England.

Coats, Michael

U.S. astronaut
Born: January 16, 1946
As spacecraft commander of STS-29, Michael Coats flew a highly successful U.S. Space Shuttle mission aboard the orbiter Discovery (March 13–18, 1989), the third following the two-and-a-half-year redesign period after the Challenger disaster of 1986. In addition to taking over 3,000 photographs of Earth, including movies, the crew members deployed a TDRS (Tracking and Data Relay System) satellite. They also performed a "heat pipe" radiator experiment, testing technology for possible use aboard the Space Station Freedom, as well as a protein crystal growth experiment and a chromosome and plant cell division experiment.

Coats also piloted Discovery, the third Shuttle to be launched in NASA's Shuttle fleet, on its first voyage, U.S. Space Shuttle Mission 41-D (August 30–September 5, 1984). During the mission he and his crew launched a record three satellites and conducted tests of a 105-foot experimental solar array. As a Navy pilot Coats had flown 315 combat missions in Vietnam.

Collins, Michael

U.S. astronaut
Born: October 31, 1930
"O.K., Eagle ... You guys take care." With those words, Michael Collins watched Neil Armstrong and Edwin "Buzz" Aldrin maneuver the Apollo 11 (July 16–24, 1969) lunar module away from the command module and begin their historic descent to the Moon. During the next 24 hours Collins continued to circle the Moon while his crew-mates made history below.

This was Michael Collins' second space flight; as pilot of Gemini 10 (July 18–21, 1966) he had made two space walks during the three-day rendezvous and docking mission.

The son of a U.S. major general, Collins was born in Rome, Italy, and is the author of *Carrying the Fire*, a book of memoirs, *Flying to the Moon and Other Strange Places*, a children's book, and *Liftoff: The Story of America's Adventure in Space*.

Congreve, Sir William

English rocket pioneer
Born: 1772
Died: 1828
Championing the use of rockets in warfare, Congreve, a colonel in the British army, made improvements to rocket designs that helped to stabilize them and make them more effective as weapons. Such "Congreve rockets" were used by the British in their bombardment of Fort McHenry (U.S.) during the War of 1812, inspiring Francis Scott Key's famous phrase, "the rockets' red glare," in the poem that would later become the American national anthem.

Conrad, Charles "Pete"

U.S. astronaut
Born: June 2, 1930
"... the dust. The dust got into everything. You walked in a pair of little dust clouds kicked up around your feet," Pete Conrad later wrote about his Apollo 12 moonwalk. It was probably the only time that it could be said that dust settled on the hyperactive astronaut.

In his four NASA missions—from his first flight on Gemini 5, in August 1965, until his last flight on Skylab 2 in May–June 1973—Conrad logged approximately 1,180 hours in space, including 14 hours of EVA (extravehicular activity). In between he commanded Gemini 11, in September 1966, which established a world altitude record at that time of 850 miles, and, as commander of Apollo 12, landed on the Moon in November 1969, spending over 30 hours romping over its surface.

It was a heady record for Pete, who after being selected by NASA in 1962, had started out as a candidate for the Mercury astronaut group, but had washed out after rebelling against the exhaustive medical testing. Taking part in the development of the Apollo lunar module, he also served as backup commander for Gemini 8 and Apollo 9.

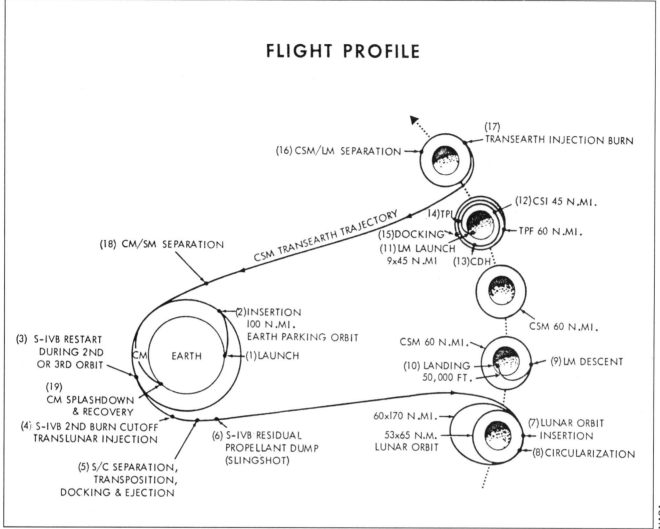

FLIGHT PROFILE

(17) TRANSEARTH INJECTION BURN

(16) CSM/LM SEPARATION

(12) CSI 45 N.MI.

14) TPI

TPF 60 N.MI.

(15) DOCKING

(11) LM LAUNCH
9x45 N.MI

(13) CDH

(18) CM/SM SEPARATION

CSM TRANSEARTH TRAJECTORY

(2) INSERTION
100 N.MI.
EARTH PARKING ORBIT

(1) LAUNCH

CSM 60 N.MI.

(3) S-IVB RESTART
DURING 2ND
OR 3RD ORBIT

CM   EARTH

CSM 60 N.MI.

(10) LANDING
50,000 FT.

(9) LM DESCENT

(19)
CM SPLASHDOWN
& RECOVERY

(4) S-IVB 2ND BURN CUTOFF
TRANSLUNAR INJECTION

(6) S-IVB RESIDUAL
PROPELLANT DUMP
(SLINGSHOT)

60x170 N.MI.

53x65 N.M.
LUNAR ORBIT

(7) LUNAR ORBIT
INSERTION

(8) CIRCULARIZATION

(5) S/C SEPARATION,
TRANSPOSITION,
DOCKING & EJECTION

NASA

A typical Apollo lunar landing mission

Cooper, Gordon

U.S. astronaut
Born: March 6, 1927
The youngest of the original "Mercury Seven" astronauts selected by NASA in 1959, Gordon Cooper made the sixth and last flight in the Mercury series (May 15–16, 1963). Cooper orbited the earth 22 times, at that time a record exceeding the combined total of all the previous Mercury missions. The self-assured and thrill-seeking Cooper, who had made NASA officials nervous by his love for racing fast cars and boats, took his first mission so much in stride that he fell

He resigned from NASA and retired from the Navy with the rank of captain in 1973. Presently he is involved in the private sector in aerospace technology.

asleep inside the spacecraft during one of the mission's almost inevitable "hold's." Cooper's second and final mission was Gemini 5 (August 21–29, 1965), with fellow astronaut Pete Conrad. The two spent eight days in space and set a record at that time of 120 revolutions around the Earth.

Cooper, who once said "I'm *planning* on getting to the Moon; I *think* I'll get to Mars," didn't get a chance to visit either. He retired from NASA in July 1970 to enter private industry.

Covey, Richard

U.S. astronaut
Born: August 1, 1946
Richard Covey was chosen to pilot the orbiter Discovery on mission STS-26 in the autumn of 1988, the first Shuttle mission (September 29–October 3, 1988)

to follow the January 1986 Challenger accident. After two and a half years of redesigning parts of the Space Shuttle, the orbiter Discovery was launched on September 29 while the world held its breath. During its four-day mission the five-member crew deployed the TDRS-C (Tracking and Data Relay Satellite) and performed several experiments onboard. The orbiter touched down smoothly at Edwards Air Force Base before thousands of onlookers. America was back in space.

With completion of this historic flight, Dick Covey had logged a total of 11 days in space.

As pilot of U.S. Space Shuttle mission 51-I (August 27–September 3, 1985), Colonel Covey, U.S.A.F., flew the mission that retrieved, repaired and redeployed a malfunctioning Leasat 3 satellite and launched three new communications satellites during its week-long space journey.

He also flew the T-38 chase plane during two early shuttle test missions, STS-2 and STS-3 in 1981 and 1982, and has served as ground-based capsule communicator (capcom) during several Shuttle missions.

Creighton, John

U.S. astronaut
Born: April 28, 1943
Pilot of U.S. Space Shuttle mission 51-G (June 17–24, 1985), Navy captain John Creighton and the seven-astronaut crew (including Saudi prince al-Saud) deployed communications and scientific satellites and ran a laser-tracking experiment for the controversial Strategic Defense Initiative during their seven days in space.

> *We proved that repairing satellites is a do-able thing. Satellite servicing is something that's here to stay.*
>
> —Robert Crippen

Crippen, Robert

U.S. astronaut
Born: September 11, 1937
The first person to pilot a manned U.S. Space Shuttle launch (STS-1, April 12–14, 1981), Robert Crippen, with Commander John Young, began the historic two-day journey on the 20th anniversary of mankind's first space flight by Soviet cosmonaut Yuri Gagarin (April 12, 1961).

An experienced pilot, Crippen had served as a carrier pilot in the Pacific and worked as an instructor for the Aerospace Research Pilot School commanded by Chuck Yeager. Trained for military space flight in

the U.S.A.F. Manned Orbiting Laboratory (MOL) Program, which was canceled in 1969, Crippen joined NASA and worked as a team leader and member of the astronaut support crew for all three Skylab missions and the Apollo/Soyuz Test Project before being transferred to the Shuttle development program.

Besides his historic first Shuttle flight aboard the Shuttle orbiter Columbia, Crippen commanded Shuttle mission STS-7 (June 18–24, 1983), which included Sally Ride, America's first woman in space, as well as missions 41-C (April 6–13, 1984) and 41-G (October 5–13, 1984). Logging over 23 days and 14 hours in his four space voyages, Crippen is NASA's "old pro" of the post-Apollo, post-Skylab era.

Crippen is currently director of the space shuttle program at NASA headquarters in Washington, DC.

Crossfield, Scott

U.S. test pilot
Born: October 2, 1921
The first person to fly at twice the speed of sound, Scott Crossfield likes to say he was "born to fly." It just might be true. Certainly airplanes have long been a part of Crossfield's life. While confined to bed with rheumatic fever as a child, he started building model

Ace X-15 test pilot Scott Crossfield

Courtesy Edwards Air Force Base

planes, and by age 13 had bartered for flying lessons at a local airport. After finishing high school, he was granted his private pilot certificate and shortly afterwards went to work for Boeing Aircraft putting together real planes on Boeing's assembly line. Earning his Navy pilot wings from the naval aviation cadet school in 1942, he spent the years during World War II as a flight instructor in Texas and after the war attended the University of Washington, receiving a master's degree in aeronautical engineering.

Crossfield started down the path to fame in 1950 when he joined NACA, the National Advisory Committee for Aeronautics. NACA, which would later become NASA, the National Aeronautics and Space Administration, was doing work in experimental aircraft, and Crossfield signed on as a test pilot. Working out of Edwards Air Force Base deep in the Mojave Desert in California, Crossfield quickly established a reputation as one of America's top test pilots.

Flying such advanced aircraft as the X-1, America's first rocket plane, Crossfield developed a friendly rivalry with Charles "Chuck" Yeager, the first person to fly the X-1 at the speed of sound. The rivalry led to an undeclared race between Crossfield and Yeager to see who would be the first to break Mach 2 (twice the speed of sound). Crossfield became the first person in history to reach that speed in November 1953, not in the specially developed X-1, but instead in a Douglas D-558-1 Skyrocket test plane hastily upgraded for the purpose.

Leaving NACA for North American Aviation in 1955, Crossfield became instrumental in the development of America's most advanced rocket plane, the X-15. As engineer and test pilot he was inseparable from the plane, the pride of North American until it was turned over to NASA in 1960. During that time Crossfield had flown the X-15 in 14 of its 30 test flights for North American, including its first "captive flight" attached to the wing of a B-52 "mother ship," its first glide flight, and its first powered flight.

Under NASA's test flights after 1960, the X-15 would go on to become the most famous aircraft in history, reaching to altitudes of over 60 miles and speeds of over Mach 6 (4,520 miles per hour), qualifying some of its pilots for Air Force astronaut wings.

But Crossfield, under frustrating orders during his North American flights, was never allowed to push the plane to those limits.

Crossfield left North American in 1967 and he is now a staff member of the U.S. House of Representatives Committee on Science, Space and Technology. He is the author of an autobiography, *Always Another Dawn,* published in 1960.

Cunningham, Walter
U.S. astronaut
Born: March 16, 1932
One of the Apollo astronauts "who didn't get there," Cunningham was a member of the crew of Apollo 7, the first manned Apollo test flight (October 11–22, 1968). During the mission Cunningham and his fellow astronauts, Walter "Wally" Schirra and Donn Eisele, ran rendezvous exercises, space systems tests and propulsion tests to gather experience and information for the later Apollo missions that would attempt to reach the Moon. The Apollo 7 crew also had the distinction of winning a special television Emmy Award for its transmissions to Earth. If their earthbound viewers had also realized that despite their exuberant television presentations the entire crew was also suffering from the first serious case of head colds in space, the trio might have won acting awards for their apparent good humor while feeling absolutely miserable.

Cunningham resigned from NASA in 1971 to enter private industry. He has written a book on his experiences as an astronaut, *The All-American Boys,* published in 1977.

D

Dana, William
U.S. test pilot
Born: November 3, 1930
Dana, who made over 16 flights in the X-15, the U.S. experimental rocket plane, was born in Pasadena, California. After attending the U.S. Military Academy at West Point, where he earned a bachelor of science

degree in 1952, Dana went into the Air Force, earning his M.S. in aeronautical engineering from the University of Southern California in 1958. Going to work for NASA as a research and test pilot, he joined the X-15 program in 1965. Dana twice flew to an altitude of over 50 miles in the X-15, qualifying him as an Air Force astronaut.

Debus, Kurt Heinrich
German rocket pioneer
Born: November 29, 1908
Died: October 10, 1983

A member of Germany's Peenemünde rocket group, Debus was brought to the United States in 1945 and began work for the U.S. government. After becoming a naturalized citizen in 1959, he joined NASA in 1960 as director of its Launch Operations Center. He later served as director of the John F. Kennedy Space Flight Center in Florida, where he oversaw the creation of the spaceport and directed the center during the Apollo missions and the three manned missions aboard Skylab, the first U.S. space station, retiring from NASA in 1974. Debus died at the age of 74 in 1983.

Demin, Lev
Soviet cosmonaut
Born: January 11, 1926

Flight engineer Lev Demin flew aboard the Soyuz 15 mission to Salyut 3 (August 1974) with fellow cosmonaut Gennady Sarafanov. When an automatic docking system failed, their scheduled month-long stay at the space station was aborted and they were forced to make an early return to Earth. The mission was Demin's only space flight.

Dixon, Thomas F.
U.S. rocket designer
Born: March 15, 1916

A pioneer in rocket design, Thomas Dixon got in on the ground floor of what would later become the Rocketdyne Division of the North American Aviation Company, where he served as vice president of research and engineering from 1955 to 1961. After briefly interrupting his career in the rocket industry to serve as deputy associate administrator of NASA, he returned to the private sector in 1963. Dixon was awarded the Robert H. Goddard Memorial Award by the American Rocket Society in 1957.

Dobrovolsky, Georgy
Soviet cosmonaut
Born: June 1, 1928
Died: June 30, 1971

At 43, Lieutenant Colonel Georgy Dobrovolsky was in command of the Soviet Soyuz 11 mission when he and fellow cosmonauts Viktor Patsayev and Vladislav Volkov became the first space travelers to be killed in space. Dobrovolsky and his crew had just successfully completed more than three weeks aboard the world's first space station, Salyut 1, and were returning home

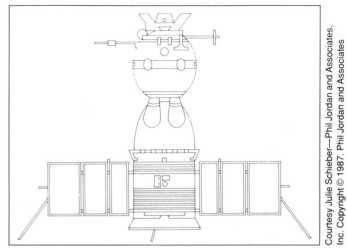

The Soyuz spacecraft

when tragedy struck. Soyuz 11 had successfully disengaged from the space station and was preparing to separate from its instrument module when a malfunction in the charges used for the separation caused all the charges to fire at once, rather than sequentially. The explosive shock tore open a seal inside one of the craft's pressure-equalization valves, causing the spacecraft's oxygen-nitrogen atmosphere to be sucked out into space. Dobrovolsky and his crew, confident of success, had flown without space suits. The three men gasped for breath and indications were that they attempted to reach the valve and close it manually, but in less than a minute Soyuz 11 was a vacuum chamber, silent and lifeless. Dobrovolsky, buried in the Kremlin wall, is the subject of a biography published in 1977, *The Flight Continues.*

Do you realize what we accomplished today? Today the spaceship was born.
—Walter Dornberger at the first successful launch of the A-4 (V-2) rocket

Dornberger, Walter
German rocket pioneer
Born: September 6, 1895
Died: June 1980

Forbidden by treaty to manufacture guns or other weapons after World War I, the German military found a loophole that would permit it to investigate the use of rockets as military weapons. The man put in charge of rocket research was a young recently graduated engineer, Walter Dornberger. An army officer, Dornberger set up an experimental station at Kummersdorf, Germany, and began research. By

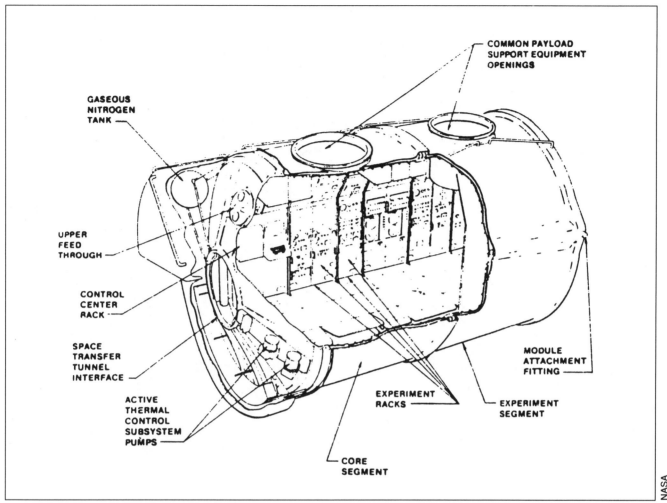

COMMON PAYLOAD
SUPPORT EQUIPMENT
OPENINGS

GASEOUS
NITROGEN
TANK

UPPER
FEED
THROUGH

CONTROL
CENTER
RACK

SPACE
TRANSFER
TUNNEL
INTERFACE

ACTIVE
THERMAL
CONTROL
SUBSYSTEM
PUMPS

EXPERIMENT
RACKS

MODULE
ATTACHMENT
FITTING

EXPERIMENT
SEGMENT

CORE
SEGMENT

NASA

The European Space Agency's Spacelab fits into the Shuttle cargo bay, where mission specialists like astronaut Bonnie Dunbar can reach it through a tunnel from the crew quarters

1932, after a number of failures, his team produced its first rocket motor and by late 1934 had fired two 3,300-pound rockets into the air. Dornberger, by then a devoted rocket enthusiast himself, had convinced Adolf Hitler to support the project and moved the team to Peenemünde, a small North Sea fishing village. There, under the leadership of Dornberger and Wernher von Braun, the notorious V-2 rocket was developed. After raining a V-2 storm of death and destruction on England during World War II, Dornberger joined with von Braun and other Peenemünde rocket scientists in surrendering to the American army in 1945. Brought secretly to America in a maneuver known as Operation Paperclip, Dornberger joined von Braun in his rocket research for the United States government. He later entered private industry and designed prototypes for the later aborted X-20 Dyna- Soar spaceplane program, among other projects.

Dryden, Hugh L.

U.S. research scientist and administrator

Born: July 2, 1898

Died: December 2, 1965

Although he had never flown an airplane, Hugh L. Dryden was one of the world's great authorities in aeronautics. A graduate from Johns Hopkins University in 1917, Dryden pioneered a series of high-speed flight phenomena projects for the National Bureau of Standards in the mid-1930s and by 1938 had become chief physicist of the agency. After leaving the Bureau of Standards in 1947 he became director of aeronautical research for NACA (the National Advisory Committee on Aeronautics) in 1947, and when that agency became NASA in 1958, Dryden was named deputy administrator.

Over his long career Dryden published over 100 papers on aeronautics research and was the recipient

TASS from SOVFOTO

Soviet cosmonaut Vladimir Dzhanibekov (left) with Mongolian cosmonaut Jugderdemidyn Gurragcha during training for their Soyuz 39 flight

of many awards, including the Daniel Guggenheim Medal in 1950 and the Wright Brothers Memorial Trophy in 1955. The Dryden Flight Research Center (formerly known as the High Speed Flight Station), at Edwards Air Force Base in California is named in his honor.

Duke, Charles

U.S. astronaut
Born: October 3, 1935
Apollo 16 (April 16–27, 1972) was Charles Duke's only space flight, but on that mission he became the 10th human to walk on the Moon. As lunar module pilot, Duke, along with Commander John Young, spent almost three days exploring the Moon's surface by foot and on the specially built Lunar Rover vehicle. He resigned from NASA in 1975 to enter private industry.

Dunbar, Bonnie

U.S. astronaut
Born: March 3, 1949
As scientific mission specialist aboard U.S. Space Shuttle mission 61-A/Spacelab D1 (October 30–November 6, 1985), Bonnie Dunbar, who had earned her Ph.D. in biomedical engineering in 1983, performed scientific experiments that were designed and controlled by the Federal German Aerospace Research Establishment and the European Space Agency. Six of the record eight person crew split up into two shifts—the Blue Team, which included Dunbar, and the Red Team—to tend the 76 experiments around the clock in the pressurized laboratory module. The West European experimenters supervised their $64 million project from a ground control center near Munich.

Also holding degrees in ceramic engineering, Dunbar went to Harwell Laboratories in Oxford, England, as visiting scientist in 1975, and subsequently worked as senior research engineer at Rockwell International Space Division on the thermal protection system for the Space Shuttle. She began working for NASA at Johnson Space Center in 1978, becoming an astronaut candidate in 1980. A private pilot and a T-38 jet copilot, Dunbar has logged over 500 hours of flying time. She also teaches mechanical engineering at the University of Houston.

Dyson, Freeman
English-American physicist
Born: December 15, 1923
Graduating from Cambridge in 1945, Dyson became an American citizen in 1951 and taught at Cornell University before joining the Institute for Advanced Study at Princeton University in 1953. A free-wheeling, adventurous thinker, Dyson has done major work in quantum electrodynamics but is best known for his challenging speculations on space science and the possibility of super-intelligent extraterrestrials. Always thought-provoking and often controversial, Dyson's carefully reasoned ideas, although sometimes appearing to be "outlandish," command serious attention and debate.

Dzhanibekov, Vladimir
Soviet cosmonaut
Born: May 13, 1942
Veteran of five different space missions from 1978 to

1985, Vladimir Alexandrovich Dzhanibekov is unquestionably one of the most experienced and brightest Soviet cosmonauts. His expert piloting of Soyuz spacecraft accounted for five out of five docking successes at a time when the Soviet space program was haunted with a one-in-four failure rate.

Dzhanibekov's most spectacular success was docking the Soyuz T-13 craft with the dead Salyut 7 space station in 1985. Drifting aimlessly and out of touch with ground control, Salyut 7 could not provide the range and radar data the docking crew ordinarily would depend on for a safe link-up. It was a tricky and exacting mission requiring unusual expertise, and Dzhanibekov and flight engineer Viktor Savinykh got the job. After a June 6, 1985 launch and two days chasing the dead station, link up they did, succeeding within a few days in repairing the station's on-board systems. On August 2, in a 6.5-hour space walk, they installed new solar panels, and within a few weeks Salyut 7 was operable again. A relief crew arrived September 18 for a long-term mission, sending Dzhanibekov back to Earth on September 27, while Savinykh stayed on.

Praised by French spationaut Jean-Loup Chrétien for his calm during a serious docking problem in an earlier flight aboard Soyuz T-6 in 1982, Dzhanibekov also piloted Soyuz 27 in 1978, Soyuz 39 in 1981, and Soyuz T-12 (attempting to repair the Salyut 7 power system in a space walk with Svetlana Savitskaya) in 1984.

He is also a deputy in the Uzbek soviet.

E

Nobody and nothing under the natural laws of this universe impose any limitations on man except man himself.
—Krafft A. Ehricke
in *Life* magazine,
January 6, 1958

Ehricke, Krafft A.
German rocket engineer
Born: March 24, 1917
Died: December 11, 1984
A visionary who became fascinated with space after seeing the motion picture *The Girl in the Moon* in Berlin in 1929, Krafft Ehricke decided at age 12 to

spend the rest of his life studying his newfound subject. His study at the Technical University of Berlin was interrupted by the outbreak of World War II, and Ehricke found himself drafted and assigned to Peenemünde, the military base where the V-2 rocket was developed.

As the war ended, Ehricke joined with Wernher von Braun and others in abandoning the base, but instead of surrendering to the Americans with others in the Peenemünde group, Ehricke traveled by foot to Berlin to rejoin his wife, Ingeborg. Brought to the United States later to join von Braun and the others, first at El Paso and later at Huntsville, Ehricke became chief of the gas dynamics section at the Army's Redstone Arsenal.

As he pursued his interest in the peaceful uses of space, he later wrote papers on rocket technology, satellite orbits and space stations. In 1954 Ehricke joined Convair, a division of General Dynamics Corporation, and became instrumental in the development of the Atlas and Centaur rockets. He later became scientific adviser to Rockwell International Corporation, builders of the Apollo spacecraft and Space Shuttle. As chair of the American Rocket Society's space flight technical committee Ehricke urged the formation of a nonmilitary, top-level astronautical research and development agency—the agency that was to become NASA. In 1959 he published the first of his three-volume work *Space Flight: Environment and Celestial Mechanics.*

Eisele, Donn

U.S. astronaut
Born: June 30, 1930
Died: December 2, 1987
As command module pilot of Apollo 7 (October 11–22, 1968), the first manned Apollo flight, Donn Eisele was one-third of the Emmy Award-winning "Wally, Walt, and Donn Show," the first live TV broadcast from space. Circling above the Earth once every 90 minutes, Eisele, Cunningham and Schirra checked out the Apollo spacecraft and Jupiter 1-B launch vehicle for safety and reliability. It was the first Apollo launch after the deaths of Virgil "Gus" Grissom, Roger Chaffee and Edward White in the Apollo 1 launchpad fire, and, aside from the Apollo 7 crew's public relations feats, the mission was tense even though it went smoothly. As navigator, Eisele's prime task was to check out the craft's intricate navigation and guidance systems.

The Apollo 7 crew acquired the dubious distinction of coming down with the first head colds in space thanks to Eisele, who was the first to catch cold. In a dramatic demonstration of the spread of the common cold, Eisele's crew-mates were taken ill immediately.

After Apollo 7, Eisele served on the Apollo 10 backup crew, but in 1972 he retired from NASA and from the Air Force, with the rank of colonel, to become a U.S. Peace Corps director in Thailand. Later, he entered the private sector.

England, Anthony

U.S. astronaut
Born: May 15, 1942
At age 25 Anthony England became the youngest

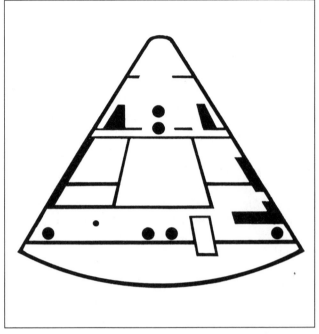

The Apollo command module provided quarters and a reentry vehicle for the three crew members during Apollo flights to the Moon.

person ever to be selected by NASA for astronaut training. As a scientist-astronaut he trained for a hoped-for assignment on an Apollo lunar landing mission, but resigned from NASA in August 1972 when budget cuts brought the Apollo program to an abrupt end. Spending the next seven years with the U.S. Geological Survey, England led expeditions to Antarctica and served on several committees studying antarctic policy.

Later returning to NASA as a senior scientist-astronaut and mission specialist aboard Spacelab 2/Shuttle mission 51-F, (July 29–August 6, 1985) England spent seven days conducting experiments in astronomy, solar physics and Earth resources observation. Although the mission was initially plagued with difficulties, the experiments went extremely well, with chief mission scientist Eugene W. Urban announcing at mission's end, "Everyone has collected tantalizing new data. It's going to take a long time before this data is analyzed and really fully appreciated. We've made some interesting new observations, and some have been very spectacular."

Prior to his flight, England had also helped develop the computer software for the U.S. Space Shuttle. He now works for the National Science Foundation.

Engle, Joe

U.S. astronaut
Born: August 26, 1932

A top aviator with 16 flights under his belt in the rocket-powered X-15 research craft, Joe Engle flew the U.S. Space Shuttle "Enterprise" in its series of approach and landing tests at Edwards Air Force Base in 1977. Although his first space flight in the U.S. Space Shuttle STS-2 (November 12–14, 1981) took him into space on board a shuttle for the first time, he had already qualified as a U.S.A.F. astronaut by flying the X-15 on three flights greater than 50 miles high—space, by Air Force standards at that time. Engle's second Shuttle command was mission 51-I (August 27–September 3, 1985), which deployed two satellites and repaired one already in orbit. By the time he resigned from NASA and retired from the Air Force in 1986, Engle had amassed over 11,400 hours of flying time in over 140 different types of aircraft.

Esnault-Pelterie, Robert

French aeronautical engineer
Born: November 8, 1881
Died: December 6, 1957

A French aviation pioneer, Robert Esnault-Pelterie became interested in rocketry in middle age. In 1927, Esnault-Pelterie and banker André Louis Hirsch established a 5,000-franc prize to be awarded annually for the best technical book on astronautics (the REP-Hirsch Award). The first award went to the German rocket pioneer Hermann Oberth in 1928. In 1930, Esnault-Pelterie published his own classic, *L'Astronautique*, still regarded as a major work in the history of astronautics. Elected to the French Academy of Sciences in 1936, he was working on development of a gasoline and liquid-oxygen fueled rocket motor

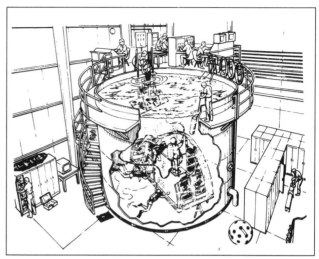

Floating in water provides the best simulation of weightlessness we can achieve on Earth. So Shuttle astronauts train in a giant vat of water called the "neutral buoyancy trainer"

when the German occupation cut his research short and forced his retirement in 1940.

Evans, Ronald

U.S. astronaut
Born: November 10, 1933

In the position some have called "the forgotten man"—certainly the loneliest part of an Apollo mission—Ronald Evans was command module pilot on Apollo 17, launched on December 7, 1972. In this last manned Moon mission, Evans, like other command module pilots before him, orbited the Moon alone for three days, conducting experiments and waiting, while his fellow astronauts Eugene Cernan and Harrison "Jack" Schmitt explored the mysteries of the Moon's surface.

F

Fabian, John

U.S. astronaut
Born: January 28, 1939

As mission specialist aboard the U.S. Space Shuttle flights STS-7, (June 18–24, 1983), and mission 51-G, (June 17–24, 1985), John Fabian took part in the launching of communications satellites. In January 1986, Colonel Fabian became director of space

programs at the U.S. Air Force headquarters in the Pentagon.

Faris, Muhammed

Syrian cosmonaut-researcher
Born: 1951

The first Syrian in space (July 22–July 30, 1987), Faris spent six days aboard the Soviet space station Mir after being launched aboard the Soyuz TM-3 spacecraft.

A Syrian air force pilot, Faris was one of two Syrians, with Munir Habib, to be trained for the mission in the Soviet Union's Star City complex.

Farkas, Bertalan

Hungarian cosmonaut-researcher
Born: August 2, 1949
The first Hungarian citizen to make a space flight, Bartalan Farkas, a skilled air force pilot, was a cosmonaut-researcher aboard Soyuz 36 (May 1980).

Feoktistov, Konstantin

Soviet cosmonaut
Born: February 7, 1926
Soviet engineer Konstantin Feoktistov was a member of the first crew to fly in space aboard a Voskhod spacecraft (October 1964). Feoktistov, who had worked with the genius of the Soviet space program, chief designer Sergei Korolev, in creating the Voskhod spacecraft, was also active in the design of the Salyut space station, the Soyuz T transport and the Progress vehicle.

Filipchenko, Anatoly

Soviet cosmonaut
Born: February 26, 1928
The author of a book *Safe Orbits* (1978), Anatoly Filipchenko was commander of Soyuz 7 (October 1969) and Soyuz 16 (1974) space flights, the latter in preparation for the Apollo/Soyuz Test Project.

Fisher, Anna

U.S. astronaut
Born: August 24, 1949
Anna Fisher knew from childhood that she wanted to become an astronaut and recognized that medical doctors would be needed on future space missions. She took her M.D. in 1976 and qualified as a mission specialist for the U.S. Space Shuttle in 1979. As a member of the crew of U.S. Space Shuttle mission 51-A in November 1984, Fisher operated the remote manipulator arm, aiding fellow astronauts Joe Allen and Dale Gardner in salvaging two malfunctioning satellites. She is married to astronaut William Fisher.

NASA

Astronaut Anna Fisher and her husband, astronaut William Fisher, sharing mission control duties at the capsule communicator console during Shuttle mission STS-8

Fisher, William

U.S. astronaut
Born: April 1, 1946
Flying aboard U.S. Space Shuttle mission 51-I (August 27–September 3, 1985), Fisher and fellow astronaut James van Hoften performed two long EVAs (extravehicular activities) for a total of 13 hours of "outside-the-craft" repair work on the malfunctioning Leasat 3 satellite. William Fisher, a medical doctor, is married to astronaut Anna Fisher, also a physician.

Fletcher, James

U.S. space administrator
Born: June 5, 1919
Administrator of NASA for two separate terms, James Fletcher served as the fourth NASA head from April 1971 to May 1977 and then became the seventh head of the agency in May 1986, following the Challenger Shuttle disaster in January of that year. Fletcher began his career as a research physicist in 1940 with the U.S. Navy Bureau of Ordnance. As a research scientist he has developed patents in sonar devices and missile guidance systems and has served on many government-industry committees, as well as the influential

President's Science Advisory Committee. He resigned as administrator in April 1989.

Friedman, Herbert

U.S. pioneer rocket astronomer
Born: June 21, 1916
After studying physics at Brooklyn College, Friedman went on to do his graduate work at Johns Hopkins University in 1940. After joining the U.S. Naval Research Laboratory, he became involved in rocket astronomy during World War II and after the war was primarily concerned with radar detection devices and solar physics. In 1949 he directed a team that sent a V-2 rocket carrying scientific instruments into space, proving in the process that X-rays did emanate from the Sun. During this same period, Friedman did pioneering work in ultraviolet mapping. Beginning in 1956 Friedman began working with Vanguard satellites to continue his studies of X-rays and ultraviolet radiation from the Sun. In 1960 he made the first X-ray photographs of the Sun and made observations proving that neutral hydrogen is present throughout the Solar System. Friedman was elected to the National Academy of Sciences in 1960 and has been awarded over 40 patents in the field of rocket and satellite astronomy. Recipient of the 1987 Wolf Prize in Physics, Friedman is now retired from his position of Superintendent of Space Science at the U.S. Naval Research Laboratory.

Frosch, Robert

U.S. space administrator
Born: May 22, 1928
The fifth Administrator of NASA, Frosch headed the agency from June 21, 1977 to January 20, 1981. Before coming to NASA, he was associate director for applied oceanography at Woods Hole Oceanographic Institution. He also served in the United Nations Environment Program and was assistant secretary of the Navy for research and development, among a variety of other posts in government and industry.

Fullerton, Charles

U.S. astronaut
Born: October 11, 1936
Fullerton has spent 380 hours in space, first as pilot of U.S. Space Shuttle mission STS-3 (March 22–30, 1982) and then as commander of mission 51-F (July 29–August 6, 1985). As one of the first astronauts assigned to the U.S. Space Shuttle program, he had previously been involved in the Shuttle's approach and landing tests.

Furrer, Rheinhard

German (West) astronaut
Born: November 25, 1940
A civilian payload specialist aboard U.S. Space Shuttle mission 61-A/Spacelab D1, Furrer, a physicist, participated in 76 experiments, most involving the manufacture of new metals in the space environment.

G

I am an ordinary Soviet man.

—Yuri Gagarin,
first human in space

Gagarin, Yuri

Soviet cosmonaut
Born: March 9, 1934
Died: March 27, 1968
The first human being in space, Gagarin stunned the world on April 12, 1961, when he successfully orbited the Earth. Remaining in orbit for 89.1 minutes and traveling at a velocity that reached 17,400 miles an hour, Yuri Gagarin opened the door to space travel for humans. Although in a few short years Gagarin's historic achievements would be eclipsed by a series of epic space voyages far surpassing his simple orbit of the Earth, he was truly the world's first space traveler.

The son of a carpenter born on a collective farm on March 9, 1934, in the village of Klushino, just west of Moscow, Gagarin had lived with his family under German occupation for several years during World War II. While attending industrial technical school and studying to become a factory worker, he became interested in flying and joined an amateur pilot's club. After being recommended for air force duty by one of the club's instructors, he joined the Orenburg air force school in 1955.

He served as a pilot with the Northern Fleet based north of the Arctic Circle for two years, then joined

Soviet cosmonaut Yuri Gagarin (left) and spacecraft/rocket designer Sergei Korolev relaxing with their wives in May 1961

NOVOSTI from SOVFOTO

the cosmonaut corps and began training in October 1959.

After his historic space flight Gagarin found himself a popular and inspiring speaker. As a spokesman for the Soviet space program and its many successes, he charmed listeners around the world with his simple style and humility. Appointed commander of the cosmonaut team in 1961, he became deputy director of the Cosmonaut Training Center in 1964. Yearning to get back into space, he managed to get himself assigned as a backup pilot for Soyuz 3 and had just finished training when he was tragically killed in an aircraft accident on March 27, 1968.

Today, a bronze statue of Gagarin welcomes visitors to Star City near Moscow, a symbol of the man, his accomplishment, and his hold on the hearts of the Russian people.

Gardner, Dale

U.S. astronaut
Born: November 8, 1948
A mission specialist aboard two U.S. Space Shuttle flights, STS 8 (August 30–September 5, 1983) and

mission 51-A (November 8–November 16, 1984), Dale Gardner has made his name in space salvage. During 51-A, with Anna Fisher at the Remote Manipulator System (RMS) controls on Discovery's aft flight deck, he and Joseph Allen performed exciting EVA (extravehicular activity) rescues of ailing satellites Palapa B-2 and Westar VI. During the Westar recovery, Allen used a foot restraint to balance at the end of the long RMS arm and steady the satellite, while Gardner used the Manned Maneuvering Unit (a powered backpack system) to propel himself to the other side of the stranded satellite, where he attached a "stinger" to its empty engine nozzle to stop its spinning. The two successfully retrieved both satellites from where they were stranded in uselessly low orbit. The five-member crew exulted in their success by dubbing themselves "The Ace Repo Company."

A U.S. Navy commander, Gardner is presently assigned to the U.S. Space Command in Colorado.

Gardner, Guy

U.S. astronaut
Born: January 6, 1948
A colonel in the U.S. Air Force, Guy Gardner made his first space flight as pilot of Shuttle mission STS-27 (December 2-6, 1988). Carrying a payload for the Department of Defense, this mission aboard the orbiter Atlantis completed 68 orbits of the Earth, landing successfully on a dry lakebed at Edwards Air Force Base, California.

Gardner flew 177 combat missions in Southeast Asia in 1972, later becoming a test pilot and test pilot instructor for the Air Force. Within the Earth's atmosphere he has logged over 4,000 hours flying time and 105 hours in space.

Man is needed in space. You can't do the things we have done up here with unmanned space probes. You need brains, you need minds up here that can think, that are innovative.

—Jake Garn, U.S. Senator,
after his shuttle flight in 1985

Garn, Jake

U.S. astronaut
Born: October 12, 1932
U.S. Senator from Utah, Garn stirred up some controversy when he flew as a civilian payload specialist aboard U.S. Shuttle mission 51-D in April 1985. As Republican chairman of the Senate appropriations subcommittee overseeing the NASA budget, Garn had been critical of Shuttle management, and critics of

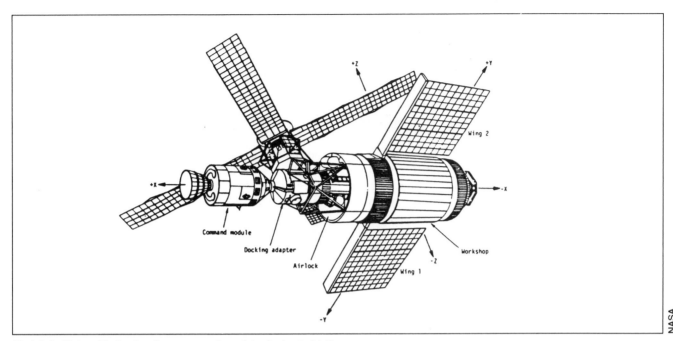

Skylab in flight with the Apollo command module docked at left

NASA charged that allowing him to fly was an effort to win him over. He was the first politician to fly in space. As a payload specialist Garn served as a test subject for space-sickness experiments.

Garneau, Marc

Canadian astronaut
Born: February 23, 1949
The first Canadian citizen to fly in space, Garneau, a commander in the Canadian Navy, flew aboard U.S. Space Shuttle mission 41-G (October 5-13, 1984). As a civilian payload specialist, he spent his eight days in space working on scientific and medical experiments designed by Canadian scientists.

Garriott, Owen

U.S. astronaut
Born: November 22, 1930
Garriott, who holds degrees in electronics engineering (a B.S. from the University of Oklahoma in 1953 and an M.S. and Ph.D. from Stanford University in 1957 and 1960 respectively), has logged almost 70 full days in space, with over 13 hours in extravehicular activity (EVA). As science pilot of Skylab 3 (July 28-September 25, 1973) he participated in the longest manned flight up to that time, and during the course of the very successful mission aided in over 300 hours of solar observations. During a rare time-off period during the mission, he also became the world's first

space barber when he trimmed the hair of fellow astronaut Alan Bean.

Garriott's second flight was as mission specialist aboard U.S. Space Shuttle mission STS-9/Spacelab 1 (November 28–December 8, 1983). In his spare time during his Spacelab mission, he broadcast communications to amateur, or ham, radio operators back on Earth.

Garriott resigned from NASA in June 1986. He has written a textbook, *Introduction to Ionospheric Physics* (1969), and over 40 scientific papers.

Gibson, Edward

U.S. astronaut
Born: November 8, 1936
As science pilot of Skylab 4, Gibson, along with fellow astronauts Gerald Carr and William Pogue, participated in the longest manned mission of the United States space program. Lasting 84 days, Skylab 4 (November 1973–February 1974) conducted observations of the Sun and Comet Kahoutek. In addition to his other duties, Gibson made three space walks lasting a total of 16 hours.

One of the first six scientist-astronauts chosen by NASA in 1965, Gibson resigned in 1974 to join the Aerospace Corporation, returning to NASA later to become chief of selection and training for new mission specialists. In 1980 Gibson resigned again to become an advanced systems manager at TRW, Inc., in Redondo Beach, California. In 1973 he published a textbook on solar physics, *The Quiet Sun.*

Gibson, Robert

U.S. astronaut
Born: October 30, 1946

Robert "Hoot" Gibson, whose nickname was inspired by an old-time cowboy star, had the misfortune to participate in two gremlin-plagued Shuttle missions. As pilot of U.S. Space Shuttle mission 41-B (February 3–11, 1984), he saw the rocket motors fail on two different satellites that were being deployed, sending both into useless orbits, while a balloon intended as a test target exploded and the Shuttle's manipulator arm malfunctioned. Gibson's second Shuttle mission had the distinction of setting a record for postponements (seven). Finally launched with Gibson as commander and Florida congressman Bill Nelson aboard as part of the seven-member crew, mission 61-C (January 12-18, 1986) was troubled by weather problems and malfunction of a package intended to observe Halley's Comet. The frustrated crew's spirits were lifted somewhat, though, when they successfully deployed an RCA communications satellite.

In 1988 he flew a third time, as commander aboard STS-27 (December 2–6), a Shuttle mission dedicated primarily to Department of Defense payloads. With completion of this third flight he has logged a total of more than 18 days in space.

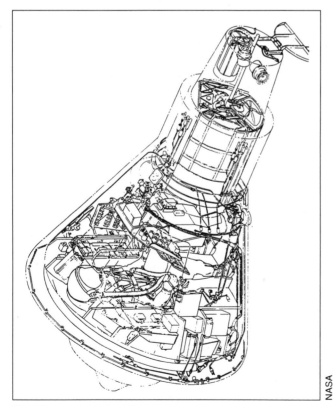

The Mercury spacecraft

Gilruth, Robert Rowe

U.S. engineer and space scientist
Born: October 8, 1913

Director of NASA's Project Mercury from 1958 to 1961 and director of the Manned Spacecraft Center (now Johnson Space Center) at Houston from 1961 to 1972, Robert Gilruth played a key role in shaping the early U.S. program for human space flight. An aerospace engineer with five doctoral degrees and numerous awards in his field, Gilruth continued to serve as a consultant to NASA after his retirement from the Manned Spacecraft Center in 1973. He was named to the National Space Hall of Fame in 1969 and the International Space Hall of Fame in 1976.

Glazkov, Yuri

Soviet cosmonaut
Born: October 2, 1939

Glazkov, the author of a popular book on space exploration, *The World Around Us* (1986), spent 19 days in space as part of the Soyuz 24 reconnaissance mission (February 1977) aboard the Soviet space station Salyut 5. Although trained in EVA (extravehicular activity) he and commander Viktor Gorbatko did not perform a space walk aboard the aging space station, but they did replace the entire Salyut atmosphere during their stay. They concluded the last mission to Salyut 5 by finishing experiments begun by the Soyuz 21 crew before them, and they returned to Earth amidst a driving snowstorm. Glazkov is also the author of a technical book, *Outside Orbiting Spacecraft*, published in 1977.

> *That was a real fireball, boy.*
> —John Glenn, watching burning debris
> fly by the window of Friendship 7

Glenn, John

U.S. astronaut
Born: July 18, 1921

The first American to orbit the Earth, John Glenn became an instant national hero at a time when America badly needed such a hero. The orbital flight of the charismatic Yuri Gagarin of the Soviet Union on April 12, 1961, had once again caused many Americans to question their nation's technological leadership, and the blow coming so soon after Sputnik (October 4, 1957) was a hard pill for Americans to swallow. A suborbital flight by Alan Shepard on May 5, 1961, had at least gotten a man into space, but Gagarin had orbited, and as heroic as the Shepard mission had been, it still seemed somehow second class. Another suborbital flight by Gus Grissom, on July 21, 1961, seemed to many almost anticlimactic.

Lifting off on February 20, 1962, in his Mercury capsule named Friendship 7, John Glenn was about to change all that. Orbiting the Earth three times over the next five hours, he became America's ticket back into the space race, its first world-class space hero.

It was a heady trip to fame for the son of an Ohio plumber. Born July 18, 1921, in Cambridge, Ohio, Glenn graduated from high school in New Concord and attended Muskingum College. Having dropped out to enter the Naval Aviation Cadet Program when World War II broke out, Glenn was soon commissioned into the Marine Corps. Assigned to Marine Fighter Squadron 155 he flew 59 combat missions. During the Korean conflict, then with Marine Fighter Squadron 311, he was credited with 63 more, also flying 27 missions as an exchange pilot with the U.S. Air Force.

After attending the U.S. Naval Test Pilot School in Maryland in 1954 he remained there as a project officer for two years. In 1957, when the National Advisory Committee on Aeronautics began studies of the effects of manned space flights on pilots, Glenn volunteered for the program and became a test subject working in centrifuge studies. Chosen as one of the original "Mercury Seven" astronauts in April 1959, he served as backup to Alan Shepard and Gus Grissom in their suborbital flights before making his own historic orbital flight in February 1962.

Glenn left NASA in 1964 to campaign for the Senate. A head injury suffered from a fall forced him to withdraw from the race, and he became an executive for a U.S. soft drink manufacturer. Defeated in a second bid for the Senate in 1970, he succeeded in 1974. A presidential contender in 1984, he withdrew before the Democratic Convention. He continues to serve in the Senate.

Glennan, T. Keith

U.S. space administrator
Born: 1905

T. (Thomas) Keith Glennan became the first administrator of the National Aeronautics and Space Administration (NASA) when it was established October 1, 1958, and served in that position until January 20, 1961, when he was replaced by James E. Webb. He came to NASA from Case Institute of Technology, Cleveland, Ohio, which he had headed since 1947. Under his direction, Case became one of the top engineering schools in the country. After leaving NASA, Glennon returned to Case and served until 1969. He served as U.S. ambassador to the Interna-

tional Atomic Energy Agency in Vienna, Austria, from 1970 to 1973.

Early in his career, after receiving a degree in electrical engineering from Yale University in 1927, Glennan was studio manager of Paramount Pictures, Inc., and Samuel Goldwyn Studios.

Glushko, Valentin

Russian rocket pioneer
Born: August 20, 1906

Valentin Petrovich Glushko began studying the problems of using reactive rocket power for space flight as early as 1917, and by 1923 he had written to Russian rocket pioneer Konstantin Tsiolkovsky about aspects of the subject. In early 1929 Glushko made a proposal to the Russian government for development of liquid propellant rocket engines, and by May of that year he had become a department head of the GDL (Gas Dynamics Laboratory), an official military research laboratory originally founded by M. K. Tikhomirov. His assignment: to work on liquid propulsion rockets. There he began his lifetime's work in earnest. He built the first experimental electrical rocket engine, explored various other fuel possibilities, investigated designs for control mechanisms and worked on numerous other theoretical and practical issues. Between 1930 and 1937 he designed more than 100 liquid-propellant rocket engines. With G. E. Langemak, Glushko coauthored *Rockets, Their Construction and Utilization*, published in 1935.

> *Dr. Goddard was ahead of us all.*
> —Wernher von Braun

Goddard, Robert

U.S. rocket pioneer
Born: October 5, 1882
Died: August 10, 1945

The "Father of American Rocketry," Robert Goddard graduated from Worcestor Polytechnic Institute in 1908. He took his Ph.D. at Clark University three years later. An instructor in physics at Princeton, 1912–1913, he joined the Clark faculty in 1914 and was associated with the university until 1943.

Fascinated with rockets all his life, he had begun testing them as early as 1908, and by 1914 had experimented with a two-stage rocket and various fuels. Highly individualistic and something of a loner, Goddard was a favorite target of the press, which saw his rocket experiments as fodder for some sensational stories. The treatment didn't help to open up

Robert Goddard with one of his rockets in his workshop at Roswell, New Mexico, October 1935

Goddard's naturally reluctant "Yankee" personality, and stories referring to him as "Moon Man" or "crackpot" embarrassed him. Actually, Goddard was a very conservative and methodical thinker, much more interested in figuring out the how's and why's of his rockets than in extraterrestrial speculations.

After receiving a grant from the Smithsonian Institution on the basis of a monograph outlining his ideas and research in 1916, he went on to publish his best-known work, "A Method of Reaching Extreme Altitudes," in 1919.

A "hands-on" experimenter, he continued his work with the use of liquid fuels for rocket propulsion throughout the '20s, settling on a combination of gasoline and liquid oxygen. After firing his first liquid-fueled rocket in March 1926, he continued to work on improvements in their design.

However, complaints from his New England neighbors and hurried visits by the local fire department every time he made a test were getting on Goddard's nerves. So in 1929, with the help of Charles Lindbergh, he received a grant from the Guggenheim Foundation and moved his equipment to a testing range in New Mexico.

Continuing to build his rockets and work on everything from combustion chambers to steering systems, Goddard launched a series of rockets from 1930 to 1935 that reached speeds of up to 550 miles an hour and heights of over a mile and a half. In a 1936 publication, *Liquid-Propellant Rocket Development*, he summarized his work up to that point. Still, the United States government showed little interest other than to seek his assistance briefly during World War II to help in developing systems for jet-assisted takeoffs (JATO) of airplanes from aircraft carriers.

Still largely unrecognized at the time of his death in 1945, he received a knowing tribute from German rocket scientist Wernher von Braun when von Braun, surprised at some of the questions put to him about rocketry after his arrival in America, asked why the questioners simply hadn't asked Goddard. "Don't you know about your own rocket pioneer?" von Braun asked. "Dr. Goddard was ahead of us all."

In 1960, United States government neglect came to an ironic end when it paid $1 million to Goddard's estate and the Guggenheim Foundation for infringements on many of the 200 patents dealing with rockets that Goddard had received during his lifetime.

And on July 17, 1969, as the Apollo 11 astronauts prepared for their historic Moon landing, the *New York Times* printed a formal retraction of its 1920 editorial ridiculing Goddard's claim that rockets would fly someday to the Moon. Today, the Goddard Space Flight Center in Maryland bears his name.

Gorbatko, Viktor

Soviet cosmonaut
Born: December 3, 1934
Despite a career haunted by medical problems—first an irregular heartbeat and later a broken ankle—Viktor Gorbatko has seen three successful space flights. Soyuz 7 (launched October 12, 1969) formed part of a three-spacecraft "space squadron" launched on successive days (intended to dock with Soyuz 8 without success, however). As commander of Soyuz 24 (February 1977), Gorbatko spent 17 days aboard Salyut 5. And, again as commander, he flew the first Vietnamese space traveler, Pham Tuan, aboard Soyuz 37 (launched July 23, 1980) to spend a week aboard Salyut 6.

It's like the old fighter pilot's life ... long periods of boredom punctuated by moments of stark terror.
—Dick Gordon, on the subject of lunar flights

Gordon, Richard

U.S. astronaut
Born: October 5, 1929
Richard "Dick" Gordon has spent approximately 316 hours in space, 2 hours and 44 minutes of that time in extravehicular activity (EVA). As pilot of Gemini

NASA

Astronaut Dick Gordon (center) checks out the Apollo 12 spacecraft with fellow crew members Charles Conrad (left) and Alan Bean

11 (September 12–15, 1966), he and fellow astronaut Charles "Pete" Conrad set a world altitude record at that time of 850 miles. Gordon was also command module pilot for Apollo 12 (November 14–24, 1969), orbiting the Moon for a day and a half while his fellow Moon travelers Pete Conrad and Alan Bean walked on the Moon's surface.

Gordon, a U.S. Navy fighter pilot and test pilot, also logged over 4,500 hours of flying time much nearer the Earth's surface. After retiring from NASA in 1972 to enter private industry, Gordon also served as a technical consultant to the television miniseries "Space" in 1984.

Grabe, Ronald

U.S. astronaut
Born: June 13, 1945
After flying over 200 combat missions in Vietnam, Ronald Grabe returned to the U.S. and attended the U.S.A.F. Test Pilot School before serving as an exchange test pilot with the Royal Air Force in the United Kingdom. Grabe was selected as a NASA astronaut candidate in May 1980 and completed his training in August 1981. He served his first NASA

flight mission as pilot of Space Shuttle mission 51-J (October 3–7, 1985) carrying a classified Department of Defense payload.

His second flight, aboard Atlantis, came nearly four years later. Grabe piloted mission STS-30 (May 4–8, 1989), during which the crew deployed the Magellan spacecraft and sent it on its way to Venus. It was the first U.S. planetary science mission to be launched since 1978. Including STS-30, Grabe has logged 195 hours in space.

Grechko, Georgy

Soviet cosmonaut
Born: May 25, 1931
Known for his jovial, easy-going manner, Grechko's long involvement with space exploration began immediately after his graduation with honors from Leningrad Institute of Mechanics in 1955, when he joined up with Sergei Korolev's rocket and spacecraft design bureau and had a hand in calculating trajectories for the first Sputnik.

Inspired by the Voskhod 1 flight of fellow engineer Konstantin Feoktistov in 1964, he also applied to join the cosmonaut team. His first flight did not come,

Soviet cosmonaut Georgy Grechko (right) with fellow cosmonaut Yuri Romanenko prior to their Soyuz 26 space flight to the Salyut 6 space station

colleague, Romanenko would have continued drifting endlessly in the vast vacuum of space, with no hope of rescue.

The two rounded out their 96-day mission, breaking the U.S. Skylab 4 crew's four-year-old space endurance record of 84 days (a record that Romanenko later went on to trounce thoroughly with a nearly year-long stay aboard Mir in 1987).

Grechko made a third space flight aboard Soyuz T-14 in September 1985, spending eight days aboard Salyut 7. He has logged a total of 134 days in space.

Gregory, Frederick

U.S. astronaut
Born: January 7, 1941

As pilot of U.S. Space Shuttle mission 51-B/Spacelab 3 (April 29–May 6, 1985), Frederick Gregory was the third black American astronaut. A colonel in the U.S. Air Force, he commanded a five-day Department of Defense mission (STS-33) in November 1989.

A graduate of Anacostia High School and the United States Air Force Academy, receiving a B.S. in 1964, Gregory earned an M.S. in information systems from George Washington University in 1977. After graduation from the Air Force Academy he became a helicopter pilot, spending three years in Vietnam. During the fall of Saigon in April 1975, he was responsible for airlifting refugees from the American Embassy to carriers offshore.

Griggs, David

U.S. astronaut
Born: September 7, 1939
Died: June 17, 1989

A captain in the Navy reserves, Dave Griggs took a walk in space during the voyage of U.S. Space Shuttle mission 51-D (April 12–19, 1985). In his unrehearsed and unscheduled extravehicular activity (EVA), Griggs and fellow crew member Jeffrey Hoffman attempted unsuccessfully to correct the failed activation of the deployed Leasat 3 satellite. Griggs logged over 148 hours in space, three of those spent in EVA. Leasat 3 was later activated successfully by the crew of Space Shuttle 51-I.

David Griggs was killed at a private airport in Arkansas, while flying a vintage World War II North American AT-6 airplane on June 17, 1989. Slated to fly again as pilot aboard Shuttle mission STS-33 a few months later, Griggs was replaced on the crew by John Blaha.

however, until Soyuz 17 (January 11, 1975), when he spent 30 days with Commander Alexei Gubarev aboard the Salyut 4 space station.

Between flights he was heavily involved with the design for Salyut 6, so when Soyuz 25 developed trouble docking on the first voyage to the new space station in October 1977, Grechko was a natural choice for the next flight. On what would become known as the "Classical Mission," Grechko (whose name means "Greek" in Ukrainian) and Yuri Romanenko (whose last name means "Roman") took Soyuz 26 up to dock at the other port. Grechko went out on an extravehicular activity (EVA) to see if he could fix what was wrong with the main port—and found everything in working order. That was the good news. Then, as he turned to look at the view, he spied Romanenko floating by, his tether accidentally unlatched! If quick reflexes had not sent Grechko grabbing swiftly for his

TASS from SOVFOTO

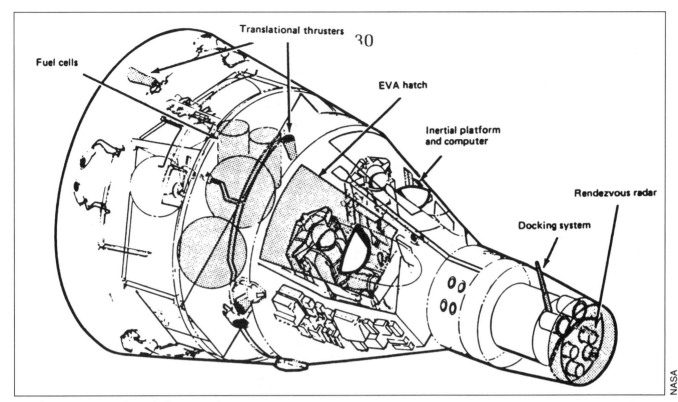

NASA

The Gemini spacecraft carried a crew of two

Do good work.
—Gus Grissom, to workers, while
touring an Atlas rocket factory

Grissom, Virgil

U.S. astronaut
Born: April 3, 1926
Died: January 27, 1967

One of the original Mercury Seven astronauts selected by NASA in April 1959, Virgil "Gus" Grissom died in America's first major space tragedy, the Apollo 1 fire on January 27, 1967.

Apollo 1 had been a tragedy waiting to happen. Grissom, who had previously flown a suborbital flight aboard Liberty Bell 7 (July 21, 1961) as part of the Mercury-Redstone series, and a Gemini flight with John Young (March 23, 1965), had been apprehensive about Apollo 1. Over 20,000 test failures of the spacecraft cabin and engines had been recorded. That did not inspire confidence, and a week before the fatal accident that took the lives of Grissom and his fellow astronauts Roger Chaffee and Edward White, Grissom had hung a lemon inside the cabin, signifying his opinion of the craft.

Tragedy struck during a normally routine simulated flight. It was sudden and deadly. With the three astronauts sealed inside the Apollo command module, a fire broke out, turning the inside of the cabin into a blazing, smoke-filled death trap, killing all three men in a matter of minutes.

A Board of Inquiry set up to investigate the accident confirmed Gus Grissom's fears. Five factors, the board found, led to the tragedy: an abundance of inflammable materials that produced toxic gases inside the cabin; poorly designed and unprotected electric cables; unprotected tubing, which contained inflammable and corrosive coolant; lack of a suitable escape system for the crew; and the unsettling fact that no fire or emergency crews were even on duty at the time of the accident.

Grissom is the subject of a biography, *Starfall*, written by his wife, Betty, and Henry Sill, and published in 1974.

Gröttrup, Helmut

German rocket engineer
Born: February 12, 1916
Died: July 4, 1981

Of the group of German rocket engineers who had developed the V-2 rocket at Peenemünde, Helmut Gröttrup was the only principal scientist to surrender to the Soviets instead of the Americans at the end of

World War II. After working for the Russians for a time in Germany, he was taken to the Soviet Union in the autumn of 1946. However, he returned to Germany in 1953, disappointed in the level of opportunity given him and feeling that his work for the Soviets had been neither appreciated nor worthwhile.

Gubarev, Alexei
Soviet cosmonaut
Born: March 29, 1931
As commander, Gubarev has piloted two successful Soyuz missions: one with Georgy Grechko in 1975 (Soyuz 17) and the other, the first multinational flight, with Vladimir Remek from Czechoslovakia three years later (Soyuz 28, March 2–10, 1978). The first mission involved a month-long stay aboard Salyut 4, while the second saw a week-long stay, again with Georgy Grechko and with Yuri Romanenko, who were doing a long-duration mission aboard Salyut 6.

Gurragcha, Jugderdemidyn
Mongolian cosmonaut-researcher
Born: December 5, 1947
Cosmonaut-researcher Gurragcha, the first Mongolian in space, spent eight days on the Soviet Soyuz 39 mission (March 22–30, 1981) to the Salyut 6 space station. Along with Commander Vladimir Dzhanibekov, he visited Vladimir Kovalenok and Viktor Savinykh, who had just begun a 74-day stay aboard Salyut. Much of the mission was spent in a resources survey of Mongolian territory. Gurragcha, a shepherd's son from northern Mongolia, had a background in communications and had studied at an aviation engineering school in the Soviet Union.

H

Haise, Fred
U.S. astronaut
Born: November 13, 1933
Fred Haise almost made it to the Moon. As part of the Apollo 13 mission (April 11–17, 1970), he had been selected to explore the Moon along with Commander James Lovell while Jack Swigert orbited overhead. In a case of "unlucky 13," though, an explosion aboard the command module forced the mission to be aborted and Haise, Lovell and Swigert made a risky return to Earth inside the cramped confines of the lunar module. The story of the three astronauts' harrowing adventure was told in the television movie "Houston, We've Got a Problem" and the book *13: The Flight That Failed* by Henry S. Cooper, Jr.

Although Apollo 13 was Haise's only space flight, he later commanded the U.S. Space Shuttle's first Approach and Landing Test Flight in August, 1977. Haise left NASA in 1979 to enter private industry.

Hart, Terry
U.S. astronaut
Born: October 27, 1946
As operator of the remote manipulator arm aboard Shuttle mission 41-C (April 6–13, 1984), Terry Hart aided fellow astronauts James van Hoften and George Nelson in helping to prove the worth of the U.S. Shuttle system by making the first satellite repair in space history. Logging nearly 168 hours in space, Hart resigned from NASA in May 1984 to return to his former employer, Bell Laboratories, in New Jersey.

Hartsfield, Henry
U.S. astronaut
Born: November 21, 1933
Prior to putting the Space Shuttle into full operation, NASA ran four test flights, with minimal crew and payload. Henry Hartsfield piloted the last orbital flight test of the U.S. Space Shuttle, STS-4, from June 27–July 4, 1982, which landed on the 15,000-foot-long concrete runway at Edwards Air Force Base to the cheers of a half-million people.

Hartsfield also commanded the first flight of the Space Shuttle Discovery (41D), August 30–September 5, 1984, and the mission 61-A/Spacelab D1 flight of October 30–November 6, 1985. Prior to his NASA service Hartsfield had been an U.S.A.F. test pilot and served in the canceled U.S.A.F. Manned Orbiting Laboratory program.

Hauck, Frederick
U.S. astronaut
Born: April 11, 1941
In January 1986 the Space Shuttle orbiter Challenger exploded seconds after lift-off, killing the seven-member Mission 51-L crew in the worst accident in

space history. More than two-and-a-half years of investigation, redesign and testing followed before the next flight was ready to go. Commanding that flight (STS-26, September 29–October 3) in the fall of 1988 was Rick Hauck, an experienced pilot and seasoned Shuttle veteran who had already logged 339 hours in space.

The flight was a resounding success. The five-member crew deployed a much-needed TDRS (Tracking and Data Relay System) satellite, performed several mid-deck experiments and touched down to a perfect landing to the cheers of thousands waiting at the desert site at Edwards Air Force Base in California. With Hauck at the helm, America was back in space.

Prior to STS-26 Hauck commanded U.S. Space Shuttle mission 51-A in November of 1984. During that mission he and his crew proved that the Shuttle could be used to salvage damaged satellites when astronauts Joe Allen and Dale Gardner captured two malfunctioning communications satellites and stowed them in the Shuttle's cargo bay.

Hauck also served as pilot in the STS-7 mission that carried the first American woman astronaut, Sally Ride, in June 1983.

Before the mission was cancelled in the Challenger aftermath, Hauck had been scheduled to command the 1986 mission that would have set the Ulysses spacecraft on its way. Hauck was a U.S. Navy test pilot prior to becoming an astronaut for NASA. He left NASA in March 1989 to become director of U.S. Navy space systems.

Hawley, Steven

U.S. astronaut
Born: December 12, 1951
The son of a minister, Steven Hawley has been a mission specialist on two U.S. Space Shuttle missions, mission 41-D (August 30–September 5, 1984) and mission 61-C (January 12–18, 1986). Hawley, who received his Ph.D. in astronomy and astrophysics from the University of California at Santa Cruz in 1977, married fellow astronaut Sally Ride in 1982. They were divorced in 1987 and he has since remarried.

Henize, Karl

U.S. astronaut
Born: October 17, 1926
As one of 11 scientist-astronauts selected by NASA in August 1967, Karl Henize waited a long time for his first flight—nearly 18 years. He made his first flight aboard U.S. Space Shuttle mission 51-F (July 29–

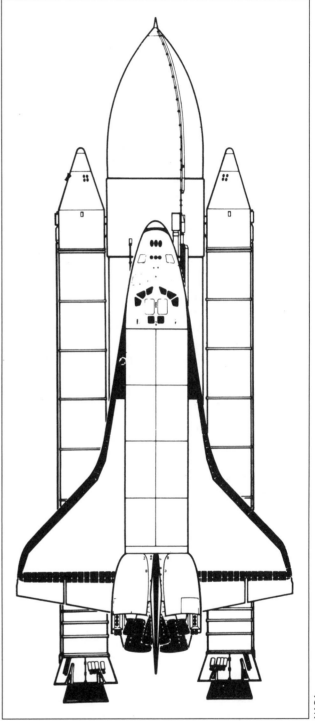

NASA

Ready for lift-off: The U.S. Space Shuttle with its giant external tank and twin solid rocket boosters attached

August 6, 1985). At 58 years and 8 months, he was the oldest person to make a space flight. During years of budget cutbacks and indecision, he patiently stayed with NASA, working on the support crew and as capcom (capsule communicator) for the Apollo 15

37

lunar landing and for all three Skylab missions, while watching others of his group begin to drift away.

A professional astronomer, Henize began as an observer for the University of Michigan at their facility in South Africa in 1948. He returned to the U.S. in 1951 and became a Carnegie post-doctoral fellow at the Mount Wilson Observatory in Pasadena, California, in 1954. His long association with space exploration began in 1956 when he joined the Smithsonian Astrophysical Observatory and established a 12-station global network for artificial Earth satellite tracking.

After his long-awaited flight, he left the astronaut ranks to become a senior scientist in the Space Science Branch at NASA's Johnson Space Center.

He is the author or coauthor of over 70 scientific papers.

Hermaszewski, Miroslaw

Polish cosmonaut-researcher
Born: September 15, 1941
Cosmonaut-researcher Hermazewski accumulated eight days in space with Soviet Commander Pyotr Klimuk on the Soviet Soyuz 30 mission to Salyut 6, where the two joined Alexandr Ivanchenkov and Vladimir Kovalenok on June 28, 1978. Klimuk and Hermazewski returned to Earth after a week-long visit, leaving Ivanchenkov and Kovalenok to continue their long-duration stay aboard the space station.

Hilmers, David

U.S. astronaut
Born: January 28, 1950
Originally scheduled, like Frederick Hauck, to fly on

the 1986 Ulysses mission that was canceled after the Challenger accident, Lieutenant Colonel David Hilmers was chosen to fly as mission specialist aboard the first post-Challenger mission, Discovery mission STS-26 (September 29–October 3, 1988). While in space Hilmers and his crew mates deployed the TDRS-C (Tracking and Data Relay Satellite) and completed several other experiments. They landed four days later at Edwards Air Force Base in California, jubilant and triumphant. Two-and-a-half years after the Challenger accident America was back in space and an age of anguish had come to an end.

No stranger to Shuttle firsts, Hilmers was also mission specialist aboard U.S. Space Shuttle mission 51-J (October 3–7, 1985), the maiden launch of the orbiter Atlantis, which launched two U.S. Department of Defense satellites.

Hoffman, Jeffrey

U.S. astronaut
Born: November 2, 1944
Jeffrey Hoffman spent three hours and 40 minutes in extravehicular activity (EVA) time while aboard U.S. Space Shuttle mission 51-D (April 12–19, 1985). Hoffman and fellow astronaut David Griggs attached a makeshift "flyswatter" to the end of the Shuttle's remote manipulator arm in an attempt to activate the deployed Leasat 3 satellite. Although the "flyswatter" was attached successfully, the satellite still couldn't be activated and had to wait for a later Shuttle mission to be correctly orbited.

Irwin, James

U.S. astronaut
Born: March 17, 1930
A popular public speaker and the founder of the High Flight Foundation, a nonprofit religious organization, James Irwin, who spent almost three days on the surface of the Moon in 1971, most recently has led five expeditions to Mount Ararat in Turkey, searching for the remains of Noah's Ark. Irwin, who says that he experienced a religious revelation during his Apollo

15 (July 26–August 7, 1971) flight, resigned from NASA on July 1, 1972.

Born in Pittsburgh, Pennsylvania, Irwin grew up at various locations around the United States and graduated from East High School in Salt Lake City, Utah. He attended the U.S. Naval Academy at Annapolis, receiving a B.S. in 1951. After earning an M.S. in aeronautical engineering and instrumentation engineering from the University of Michigan, he entered the U.S. Air Force, serving as a fighter pilot.

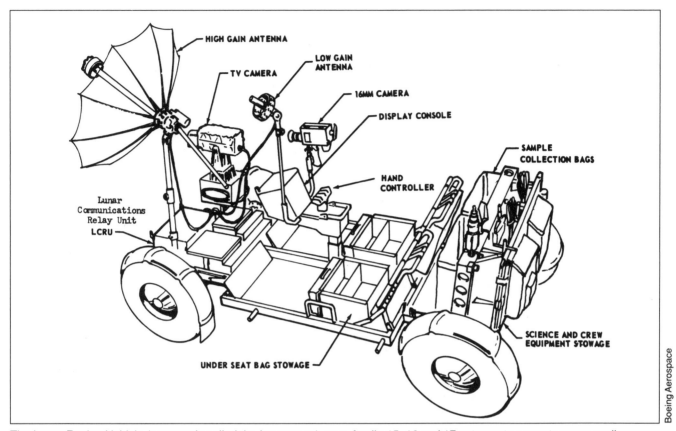

Boeing Aerospace

The Lunar Roving Vehicle (commonly called the lunar rover) gave Apollo 15, 16 and 17 astronauts a way to move easily across the Moon's surface

He joined NASA in 1966, where he worked testing lunar module systems and served on the support crew for Apollo 10.

As lunar command module pilot for Apollo 15, Irwin and fellow astronaut David Scott were the first astronauts to make use of the Lunar Rover, an electric car that carried them over 18 miles on three Moon excursions lasting a total of 21 hours.

Irwin is the author of *To Rule the Night*, published in 1973. The book discusses his life as an astronaut and his spiritual conversion.

Ivanchenkov, Alexandr

Soviet cosmonaut
Born: September 28, 1940
Ivanchenkov has served as flight engineer on two Soyuz flights, Soyuz 29 (June 15–November 2, 1978) to Salyut 6 and Soyuz T-6 (June 24–July 2, 1982) to Salyut 7.

In his 140-day stay aboard Salyut 6 with fellow cosmonaut Vladimir Kovalenok, he broke the 96-day record set by Soyuz 26 cosmonauts Georgy Grechko and Yuri Romanenko. New health maintenance and exercise routines enabled them to walk away from

their spacecraft, unlike the Soyuz 26 team, showing that the Soviets had learned valuable lessons about living and working in a weightless environment. The pair also included a two-hour-plus space walk among their activities (June 29, 1978).

Ivanchenkov served as flight engineer on the first mission to include a Western European, French spationaut Jean-Loup Chrétien—Soyuz T-6. Vladimir Dzhanibekov was commander, and the three spent a week on Salyut 7 with Anatoly Berezovoy and Valentin Lebedev early in that team's marathon seven-month stay.

Ivanov, Georgy

Bulgarian cosmonaut-researcher
Born: July 2, 1940
The first Bulgarian in space, Ivanov served as cosmonaut-researcher aboard Soyuz 33 (April 10–12, 1979), which was commanded by cosmonaut Nikolai Rukavishnikov. Unfortunately, the craft developed engine trouble as it approached Salyut 6 for docking—putting an end to the mission and forcing it to head for home using a backup engine.

J

Jarvis, Gregory

U.S. astronaut
Born: August 24, 1944
Died: January 28, 1986

A Hughes Aircraft engineer, Gregory Jarvis died with six other U.S. astronauts when the Challenger shuttle blew up on January 28, 1986. Jarvis's expertise as an advanced satellite specialist had been sought for two previous shuttle missions, but he had been replaced by politicians on those flights. Aboard Mission 51-L he had planned to supervise a fluid dynamics experiment.

Jaehn, Sigmund

German cosmonaut-researcher
Born: February 13, 1937

The first German to fly in space, Sigmund Jaehn served as a cosmonaut-researcher on Soyuz 31 (August–September 1978). Jaehn, an air force pilot, had previously held an appointment at the Gagarin Air Force Academy in the Soviet Union before becoming an inspector for the general staff of the German Air Force.

K

Karman, Theodore von

Hungarian-American aeronautical engineer and physicist
Born: May 11, 1881
Died: May 7, 1963

The son of an educator, Theodore von Karman was educated at the Royal Polytechnic University at Budapest, Gottingen, and the University of Paris. After viewing an early airplane flight in Paris in 1908, he developed an interest in aeronautical engineering. Von Karman moved to the United States, accepting a post at the Guggenheim Aeronautical Laboratory at the California Institute of Technology in Pasadena, California (GALCIT). He became director the following year, and with Frank Malina in the late 1930s, he developed the laboratory into the beginnings of what is now NASA's Jet Propulsion Laboratory. A pioneer in the theories of supersonic flight, von Karman later became chief consultant on the development of the Atlas, America's first operational intercontinental ballistic missile.

Kerwin, Joseph

U.S. astronaut
Born: February 19, 1932

Science pilot on the United States Skylab 2 mission (May 25–June 22, 1973), Kerwin was the first medical doctor to do medical research while in orbit. Kerwin and his fellow astronauts, Charles Conrad and Paul Weitz, spent 28 days aboard Skylab as the first Skylab crew. During the mission they proved themselves to be expert repairmen, performing emergency repairs on the space station to make it habitable.

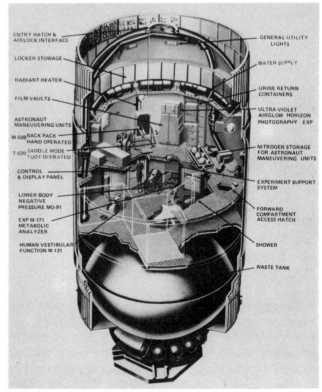

Inside the Skylab space station

Born in Oak Park, Illinois, Kerwin graduated from Fenwick High School in 1949 and attended the College of Holy Cross in Worcester, Massachusetts, where he received a B.A. in philosophy. He received his M.D. in 1957 from Northwestern Medical School in Chicago and completed his internship at the District of Columbia General Hospital in Washington, D.C. After graduating from the U.S. Naval School of Aviation at Pensacola, Florida, he became a naval flight surgeon in 1958.

One of the first six scientist-astronauts selected by NASA in 1965, Kerwin worked on the design and development of biological insulation garments worn by the astronauts on their return from the Moon flights. Before being named as a member of the Skylab 2 crew, he served as capcom (capsule communicator) for Apollo 13.

After Skylab, Kerwin became director of life sciences for the astronaut office and also participated in the development of the Space Shuttle crew station, controls and medical monitoring systems. In 1987 he retired from NASA and the U.S. Navy to go to work for Lockheed.

Khrunov, Yevgeny

Soviet cosmonaut
Born: September 10, 1933
January 15, 1969, saw Khrunov's historic transfer from one spacecraft to another with fellow cosmonaut Alexei Yeliseyev when they made a space walk from their Soyuz 5 craft to Soyuz 4. The first space travelers ever to perform this feat, the two completed it within an hour's time. Although Khrunov has remained with the Soviet space program, he has never again ventured into space himself.

Khrunov is the author of several books, including textbooks on subjects such as extravehicular activity, an autobiography (*The Conquest of Weightlessness*, 1976) and a science-fiction novel (*The Way to Mars*, 1979).

Kincheloe, Iven

U.S. test pilot
Born: July 2, 1928
Died: July 26, 1958
Soloing at the age of 14, Iven Kincheloe was once described by a friend as "a guy with flying in his bones." After graduating with a B.S. in aeronautical engineering from Purdue University, Kincheloe flew almost 100 combat missions in Korea, shooting down 10 enemy aircraft. After attending the British Empire Test Pilot School and graduating in 1954, he was

assigned to Edwards Air Force Base, where he flew the experimental X-2 rocket plane. On September 7, 1956, Kincheloe pushed the X-2 to a then record altitude of 126,200 feet.

Considered the number-one choice to fly the even more advanced X-15 rocket plane, Kincheloe's life ended tragically on July 26, 1958, when the chase plane he was flying flamed out and crashed near Edwards.

Kizim, Leonid

Soviet cosmonaut
Born: August 5, 1941
Kizim's nearly 376 days in space and over 31 hours of logged EVA time make him a space veteran to be reckoned with. He was commander of the Soyuz T-10 space flight, which was launched February 8, 1984, with fellow cosmonauts Vladimir Solovyov (as flight engineer) and Oleg Atkov (a cardiologist) aboard. They stayed aboard the Salyut 7 space station for 237 days in space.

In addition, he commanded the Soyuz T-15 spacecraft to both Salyut 7 and Mir to add another 125 days to his record. The first crew to enter Mir after its launch on February 20, 1986, Kizim and Vladimir Solovyov took up residence on March 15. On May 5, they left Mir for Salyut 7 in a historic orbit-transfer mission. Aboard Salyut 7 they built a demonstration

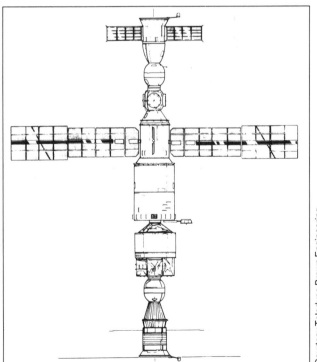

Top-down view of the Soviet Mir space station complex

Courtesy Teledyne Brown Engineering

41

TASS from SOVFOTO

Chief Soviet spacecraft designer Sergei Korolev consulting with the Voskhod 1 crew, Komarov (left), Feoktistov, and Yegorov (right)

girder during EVA outside the station, returning to Mir on June 25. A few weeks later they returned to Earth after mothballing Mir until its next visitors arrived.

Klimuk, Pyotr

Soviet cosmonaut
Born: June 10, 1942
By the age of 36 this ambitious young cosmonaut had commanded three space flights: Soyuz 13 in December 1973 (with engineer Valentin Lebedev, an eight-day astronomical mission to observe Comet Kahoutek), the 63-day Soyuz 18 mission to the Salyut 4 space station in 1975 (with Vitaly Sevastyanov) and the Soyuz 30 flight in June–July 1978 for an eight-day mission to Salyut 6 (an Intercosmos mission with Polish researcher Miroslaw Hermaszewski).

Deputy director of political affairs for the Gagarin Cosmonaut Training Center since 1978, Klimuk has been a member of the Central Committee of the Communist Party and was also a member of the Supreme Soviet from 1980–82. His autobiography, *Next to the Stars*, was published in 1979.

Knight, William

U.S. test pilot
Born: November 18, 1929
As a member of the X-15 test pilot team, William "Pete" Knight set a world record by flying the experimental rocket plane to Mach 6.7 (4,520 miles per hour) on October 3, 1967. Making 16 flights in the X-15, Knight also earned an Air Force astronaut rating by climbing the plane to a height of 280,500 feet, over 53 miles above Earth.

Born in Noblesville, Indiana, Knight attended Butler and Purdue Universities and joined the U.S. Air Force in 1952 and the Air Force Test Pilot School at Edwards AFB in 1958. After flying 253 combat missions in Vietnam he returned to the U.S. and became test director at Wright-Patterson AFB in Ohio. Later becoming vice commander of the Air Force Flight Center at Edwards, he retired as a colonel in 1982.

Komarov, Vladimir M.

Soviet cosmonaut
Born: March 16, 1927
Died: April 24, 1967

The first person to die during a space mission, Komarov plunged to his death on April 24, 1967, when the reentry parachute of his Soyuz 1 space capsule failed to deploy properly. Chosen for his skill to pilot the first manned flight of the new Soviet Soyuz spacecraft, the Soviet cosmonaut had previously piloted Voskhod 1 on October 12–13, 1964, with design engineer Konstantin Feoktistov and aerospace physician Boris Yegorov aboard. His tragic death caused a delay in further Soyuz flights for more than a year while an investigation ensued.

Komarov graduated with honors from the Soviet Air Force secondary school in 1942 and was selected for cosmonaut training in 1960. A skilled parachutist who had made over 77 jumps, Komarov had once said "whoever has flown once, whoever has piloted an airplane once, will never want to part with either an aircraft or the sky."

Komarov's biography, *Tester of Spaceships,* written by his friend and fellow cosmonaut, Vasily Lazarev, was published in 1976.

I'm only sorry that we didn't manage to send a man to the Moon during Korolev's lifetime.
—Nikita Khrushchev
in his memoirs

Korolev, Sergei Pavlovich

Soviet rocket engineer
Born: December 30, 1906
Died: January 14, 1966

The cornerstone of Soviet success in space rests in the work of Sergei Korolev, whose genius as spacecraft designer, rocket engineer and overseer of spacecraft and rocket development translated early experiments into breakthroughs throughout the Soviet program's formative years. Korolev's master touch can be seen in every Soviet space success—from the launch of Sputnik onward. Ironically, the magnitude of his contribution was kept secret for political reasons for many years until after his death in 1966.

Always interested in flight and technology, Korolev graduated from a technical school in Moscow in 1929, obtained a pilot's license and started building gliders and light planes. In 1931 he joined a group of rocket enthusiasts called GIRD (Russian acronym for Group Studying Rocket Propulsion), led by rocket pioneer Fridrikh Tsander. There he began working on theoretical and practical problems of rocket design and he built the GIRD 09 rocket designed by M.K. Tikhonravov, a hybrid (solid/liquid propellent) rocket that was tested successfully in 1933. About this time, the potential of rocket power became recognized by the military and the group received a budget. Work began in earnest, and the Soviet Union—like Germany, with rocket enthusiasts Hermann Oberth and the VfR (the German rocket society), and the U.S., with the work of Robert Goddard—began to move toward making dreams of rocket power to space come true.

In 1938, however, Korolev and his coworkers were suddenly imprisoned in the gulags, where he remained for years during Stalin's regime, his work on rocketry now politically suspect. During part of his imprisonment, Korolev was allowed to work, mostly on aviation, but, even after he left the gulag, most of his work was kept secret, not only from the world, but within the Soviet Union.

After World War II, under Korolev's supervision, military rockets were modified by 1949 for research in the upper atmosphere. Between 1949 and 1952 the Soviets began researching the effects of high-altitude flight on living organisms, rocketing dogs in recoverable nose cones as high as 60 miles (95.5 km). They were the first living creatures to fly in space. By the mid-1950s, the deeds of a nameless "Chief Designer" of rockets began to be talked of.

In the years since his death in 1966, the Soviet information ban has been lifted, and it has become clear that Korolev was the "chief designer," and that his work was critical to Sputnik's success in 1957, Vostok 1 and Gagarin's first orbit around Earth in 1961, Voskhod, Soyuz, and, most important, the rocketry that launched them all. He was a man of enormous energy, talent, engineering expertise and management ability. Nikita Khrushchev would later write in his own memoirs, "We had absolute confidence in Comrade Korolev. When he expounded his ideas, you could see passion burning in his eyes, and his reports were always models of clarity. He had unlimited energy and determination, and he was a brilliant organizer."

During a routine operation for hemorrhoids in January 1966, the surgeon discovered a cancerous tumor of the colon and decided to remove it without adequate preparation. Korolev's heart gave out and he died on the operating table at the age of 59. He was given a hero's burial; his ashes were placed within the Kremlin Wall in Moscow. It would take the Soviet space program many years to recover from the loss.

Kovalenok, Vladimir

Soviet cosmonaut
Born: March 3, 1942

Vladimir Kovalenok has spent over 216 days in space, most of them in three visits to the Salyut 6 space station. On mission Soyuz 25 (October 9, 1977), which Kovalenok commanded, bad luck forced him and cosmonaut Valery Ryumin to abort the planned 90-day mission to the space station after only two days. On Kovalenok's second try his fortunes fared better, and the Soyuz 29 mission (June 15, 1978) found Kovalenok and his fellow cosmonaut Alexandr Ivanchenkov spending over 139 days in space, most of them aboard Salyut 6. Kovalenok's third and final mission to date was aboard Soyuz T-4 (launched March 12, 1981) again to Salyut 6 for a flight lasting 75 days.

> *Man is the deciding element…As long as man is able to alter the decision of the machine, we can perform under any known conditions.*
> —Christopher Kraft

Kraft, Christopher C., Jr.

U.S. flight director
Born: February 28, 1924

The most frequently heard voice during the early years of the U.S. space program, Chris Kraft was flight director for all the Project Mercury flights and most of the Gemini missions. His was the responsibility for controlling each mission from the ground, and he decided ultimately whether to launch or not and what to do if things went awry.

Kraft began working for NACA in 1945 and in 1958 he became one of the original members of the space task group charged with developing the Mercury program. He was responsible for much of the mission and flight-control development and the design of the Mission Control Center at what is now the Johnson Space Center. Kraft also served as director of flight operations and became director of JSC in 1972, retiring in August 1982, and is now an aerospace consultant in the Houston area.

Krikalov, Sergei

Soviet cosmonaut
Born: 1958

Sergei Krikalov made his first space flight as flight engineer aboard Soyuz TM-7 (launched November 26, 1988). With Alexandr Volkov and Jean-Loup Chrétien of France also aboard, the TM-7 docked with Mir to visit long-duration cosmonauts Vladimir Titov and

Musa Manarov and physician Valery Polyakov, bringing the population of the space station to six. Krikalov stayed on with Volkov and Polyakov, while Titov, Manarov and Chrétien returned to Earth aboard Soyuz TM-6 on December 21. Four months later, after "mothballing" Mir, Krikalov, Volkov and Polyakov undocked the TM-7 for descent on April 27, 1989.

Kubasov, Valery

Soviet cosmonaut
Born: January 7, 1935

Hand picked for the cosmonaut list by the Soviet master spacecraft designer Sergei Korolev, Valery Kubasov has flown three space missions as an engineer-mechanic. He became the first human to actually attempt construction in space when he operated a prototype welding apparatus during his Soyuz 6 (October 11, 1969) flight. The dedicated and personable Kubasov found himself in the world spotlight when his next mission, Soyuz 19 (July 15, 1975), sent him and fellow cosmonaut Alexei Leonov to link up with the American Apollo 18 spacecraft in the famous Apollo-Soyuz joint mission. For his third and final flight, Kubasov commanded Soyuz 36 (May 26, 1980) in which he flew with Hungarian cosmonaut-researcher Bertalan Farkas to visit the Salyut 6 space station.

Kubasov has written a book of memoirs, *To Touch Space,* published in 1984.

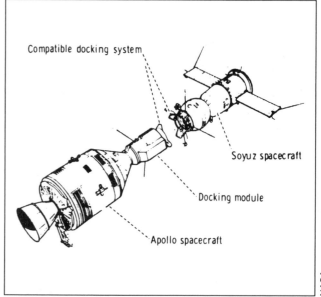

Cosmonauts and astronauts meet in orbit: During the Apollo-Soyuz Mission a Soviet Soyuz spacecraft (with cosmonauts Kubasov and Leonov aboard) docked with a U.S. Apollo spacecraft (carrying astronauts Stafford, Brand and Slayton)

Kuiper, Gerard

Dutch-American astronomer
Born: December 7, 1905
Died: December 23, 1973

Born in the Netherlands, Gerard Kuiper earned his Ph.D. at the University of Leiden. After moving to the United States in 1933, he became an American citizen in 1937. Best known for his studies of our Solar System, he had a long association with Yerkes Observatory, holding the position of director between 1947 and 1949, and returning for a second term of office from 1957 to 1960. From 1960 until his death in 1973, Kuiper worked in a similar capacity at the Lunar and Planetary Laboratory at the University of Arizona. His theories of the origins of the planets, including the idea that stars and planets are products of condensation from interstellar gas clouds, helped to spark a renewed interest in our Solar System. During the '60s and early '70s, until the time of his death, he was also closely linked with the American space program, instigating many planetary research projects.

L

Laveikin, Alexander

Soviet cosmonaut
Born: 1951

With veteran cosmonaut Yuri Romanenko, Alexander Laveikin manned the second mission to the Soviet space station Mir, arriving aboard Soyuz TM-2 on February 7, 1987. The plan was that the two would stay through the following October to break the world endurance record of 237 days established by Leonid Kizim, Vladimir Solovyov and Oleg Atkov aboard Salyut 7 in 1984.

At the end of March a 22.7 ton astrophysics module, launched by a Proton booster, headed off to dock with Mir. But after several tries to dock the module, Laveikin and Romanenko performed an extravehicular activity (EVA) on April 12 to clear away an object that had prevented a firm connection.

In June, the two performed two EVAs during which they installed a new, third solar array to add to the space station's power supply.

But by July Laveikin had become ill, possibly with a cardiovascular problem, and it was clear he would not be able to stay on. On July 22 Soyuz TM-3 headed for the rescue, launched July 22 with Muhammed Faris, a Syrian, and Soviet cosmonauts Alexander Viktorenko and Alexandr Alexandrov aboard. Laveikin returned to Earth with Faris and novice pilot Viktorenko and was whisked away by helicopter for immediate medical attention. Alexandrov stayed behind to take his place aboard Mir.

Lazarev, Vasily

Soviet cosmonaut
Born: February 23, 1938

Vasily Lazarev's future in space looked bright. For his first voyage aboard the Soviet Soyuz 12 (September 27, 1973) everything went smoothly enough and he and flight engineer Oleg Makarov flew a comfortable two-day mission. Picked to fly a second mission together, though, the two cosmonauts' luck ran out.

Vasily Lazarev's second space flight reached a height of only 90 miles, lasted only 22 minutes and almost ended in tragedy. A malfunction only minutes into the flight forced ground controllers to abort Soyuz 18-A (April 5, 1975) when the spacecraft had to be prematurely separated from its launch rocket. Lazarev and Makarov plunged back toward the Earth, suffering the agonizing pressure of nearly 18 G's before they landed on a mountainside near the Soviet-Chinese border. Although both men survived, rumors indicated that the 47-year-old Lazarev had suffered internal injuries. Although the rumors were never verified, western observers noted that the promising cosmonaut never flew again.

We have an apron all ready for you, Svetlana.
—Valentin Lebedev to Svetlana Savitskaya on her arrival on Salyut 7 in August 1982.
She retorted that she was a guest and *he* was the host

Lebedev, Valentin

Soviet cosmonaut
Born: April 14, 1942

The brooding and athletic Lebedev has flown on two Soviet space missions. During his Soyuz 13 mission (December 18, 1973) he joined Pyotr Klimuk, spending eight days in flight and making observations of Comet Kahoutek. His second mission, the Soyuz T-5 mission to the Salyut 7 space station (May 13, 1982), included visits from several cosmonauts, among them Svetlana Savitskaya, the second woman in space.

Despite the visits, though, the long mission found Lebedev and Commander Anatoly Berezovoy occasionally getting on each other's nerves as they shared the station's cramped living space for over seven months. Writing about his experiences aboard the space station later, Lebedev suggested that since both he and Berezovoy had been "worriers" and brooders, perhaps future missions should be composed of a better mixture of personality types.

Lee, Mark

U.S. astronaut
Born: August 14, 1952
A major in the U.S. Air Force, Mark Lee became an astronaut candidate in 1984 and made his first space flight some five years later as mission specialist aboard the orbiter Atlantis on Shuttle mission STS-30 (May 4–8, 1989). The five-member STS-30 crew deployed the spacecraft Magellan to begin its journey to Venus, where it would arrive in mid-1990. The first planetary mission to be deployed from the Shuttle, Magellan was also the first U.S. planetary science mission to be launched since 1978, when NASA sent Pioneer Venus 2 on its way to the same planet. Lee, who is a registered professional engineer with degrees in civil and mechanical engineering, has logged a total of 97 hours in space.

Leestma, David

U.S. astronaut
Born: May 6, 1949
Leestma, a commander in the U.S. Navy, performed a space walk with astronaut Kathryn Sullivan, America's first woman space-walker, during U.S. Space Shuttle mission 41-G (October 5–13, 1984). The two engaged in a 3.5 hour extravehicular activity (EVA) in which they demonstrated refueling techniques for satellites.

He made his second flight, this time for the Department of Defense, as mission specialist aboard Columbia, Shuttle mission STS-28 (August 8–13, 1989). Including his second flight, Leestma has logged a total of 318.5 hours in space.

Lenoir, William

U.S. astronaut
Born: March 14, 1939
As mission specialist aboard the U.S. Space Shuttle mission STS-5 (November 11–16, 1982) William Lenoir aided in the deployment of two satellites, helping to demonstrate the Shuttle's practical value as a space delivery system. One of 11 scientist-astronauts selected by NASA in 1969, Lenoir also served as backup science pilot for the Skylab 3 and Skylab 4 missions.

[I'm] soaring like a bird over a huge colored map.
—Alexei Leonov in 1965 during his historic
Voshkod 2 space walk

Leonov, Alexei

Soviet cosmonaut
Born: May 30, 1934
An accomplished artist, the personable Alexei Leonov has been on two historic space missions. During his Voskhod 2 mission (March 18, 1965) he became the first human to walk in space when he spent 10 minutes outside the spacecraft commanded by his fellow cosmonaut Pavel Belyayev. The successful Voskhod mission almost ended in disaster, though, when the cosmonauts missed their prime recovery area and were forced to land in the Ural Mountains, spending a freezing, snowy night aboard the spacecraft before rescuers could arrive.

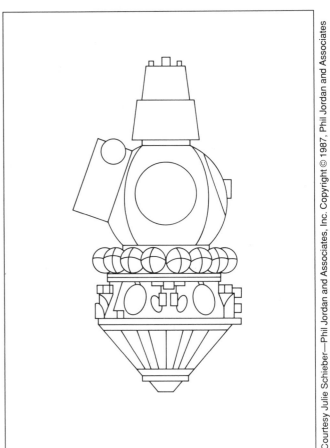

The Soviet Voskhod spacecraft

Leonov's second mission was as commander of the Soyuz half of the historic Apollo-Soyuz Test Project (July 1975), which found the American Apollo and Soviet Soyuz spacecraft linking up to share friendship and scientific experimentation in space. His flight engineer on the historic mission was Valery Kubasov, and after the mission the two Soviets joined their American counterparts in a worldwide speaking tour demonstrating the possibilities of U.S./Soviet cooperation in space. It was the last time, though, that such a joint mission was flown.

Leonov has authored several books, including *Wait for Us, Stars* (1967), *Stellar Roads* (1977) and *Life Among the Stars* (1981).

Levchenko, Anatoly

Soviet cosmonaut
Born: 1951
Died: August 6, 1988

A test pilot prior to becoming a cosmonaut in 1981, Anatoly Levchenko trained to become one of the first pilots of the Soviet space shuttle during its development. In December 1987 he flew into space for the first time during the Soyuz TM-4 mission to the Mir space station. With him were Musa Manarov and Vladimir Titov, who would relieve long-duration cosmonauts Yuri Romanenko and Alexandr Alexandrov. Levchenko returned with Romanenko and Alexandrov and, to test his ability to pilot after several days in zero gravity—as a shuttle pilot would have to do—he flew an aircraft immediately after landing. Eight months later, he died of a brain tumor.

Ley, Willy

German-American engineer and rocket pioneer
Born: October 2, 1906
Died: June 24, 1969

Born in Berlin, Willy Ley studied at the University of Berlin and was on his way to becoming a zoologist when he chanced upon an early book on rocketry. From that moment on the direction his life would take was decided. One of the founders of the German Rocket Society in 1915, he was also a writer whose popular books on rocketry captured the public's imagination. Although it was Ley who introduced Wernher von Braun into the German Rocket Society, his conscience wouldn't permit him to follow von Braun and others in the group in their collaboration with the Nazis after Adolf Hitler came into power. After coming to the United States in 1935, he became a naturalized citizen in 1944. Ironically, although Ley had tremendous influence among science-fiction writers and space buffs in the U.S., it was von Braun, bringing the United States his experience with the V-2 rocket series used by the Nazis, who became America's hope for a space future.

Although he had fought for it and dreamed about it all of his life, Ley died three weeks before Neil Armstrong and Edwin "Buzz" Aldrin made their historic touch-down on the Moon.

Lichtenberg, Byron

U.S. astronaut
Born: February 19, 1948

Serving aboard U.S. Space Shuttle mission STS-9, (November 28–December 8, 1983), as civilian payload specialist, Byron Lichtenberg became American's first nonprofessional space traveler. Trained as a Spacelab payload specialist whose primary duty was the operation of scientific instruments, Lichtenberg spent almost 11 days in space during his Spacelab flight.

Receiving a B.S. in aerospace engineering from Brown University in Boston in 1969, he later served in Vietnam, returning to college and receiving an M.S. in mechanical engineering from the Massachusetts Institute of Technology and a Ph.D. in biomedical engineering in 1979. Lichtenberg, who had wanted to be an astronaut from childhood, was turned down when he applied for the NASA astronaut group in 1977, but was selected as a civilian payload specialist in 1978.

Lind, Don

U.S. astronaut
Born: May 18, 1930

As part of U.S. Space Shuttle mission 51-B/Spacelab 3 (April 29–May 6, 1985), Lind was part of a seven-person crew performing experiments in materials processing and space medicine. A highly trained scientist with a B.S. in physics from the University of Utah, Lind earned his Ph.D. in high-energy nuclear physics from the University of California at Berkeley in 1964. A Mormon, he is the subject of an inspirational biography, *Don Lind: Mormon Astronaut*, written by his wife, Kathleen, and published in 1985.

Lounge, John M. "Mike"

U.S. astronaut
Born: June 28, 1946

John Lounge was named one of three mission specialists to fly on the first post-Challenger shuttle mission, Discovery flight STS-26 (September 29–October 3, 1988). The world watched and thousands cheered as the orbiter lifted off from the launchpad for the first time since seven astronauts had lost their lives seconds after lift-off on January 28, 1986. Lounge and his four crew-mates successfully deployed the TDRS-C (Tracking and Data Relay Satellite), completed several experiments and returned smoothly to Earth four days later, without a hitch.

Prior to STS-26, Lounge had been a veteran of one previous Shuttle flight. Serving as a mission payload specialist aboard U.S. Space Shuttle mission 51-I (August 27–September 3, 1985), Lounge operated the Shuttle's remote manipulator arm to aid fellow astronauts William Fisher and James van Hoften in capturing and repairing the ailing Syncon IV-3 satel-

lite. He also assisted in deploying the Australian Aussat communications satellite.

A lieutenant colonel in the Air Force Reserve, Lounge attended the U.S. Naval Academy and the University of Colorado, receiving a B.S. in physics and mathematics and an M.S. in astrogeophysics. He worked in the Payload Operations Division at NASA's Johnson Space Center prior to becoming an astronaut and has worked on the Shuttle Centaur program (canceled in 1986) as well as space station design development.

Lousma, Jack

U.S. astronaut
Born: February 29, 1936
As commander of the third orbital test flight of the U.S. Space Shuttle Columbia, STS-3 (March 22–30, 1982), Lousma spent eight days in space with pilot Gordon Fullerton. During that period they tested the remote manipulator arm and various Shuttle systems. Prior to his Shuttle mission Lousma had spent over 59 days in space as pilot of Skylab 3 (July 28–September 25, 1973). A Marine Corps pilot, Lousma had received a B.S. in aeronautical engineering from the University of Michigan in 1959 and a degree in aeronautical engineering from the U.S. Navy Post-Graduate School in 1965.

Lousma resigned from NASA in October 1983 to enter politics. Presently he works in private industry.

Is it inhabited?

—running joke among Apollo 8 astronauts looking back at the Earth

Lovell, James

U.S. astronaut
Born: March 25, 1928
"The moon is essentially gray, no color ... looks like plaster of Paris, sort of gray sand," is how James Lovell described the surface of the Moon during the flyby flight of Apollo 8 (December 21–27, 1968). If, in the words of science-fiction writer Robert Heinlein, "the Moon is a harsh mistress," then we might wonder if such an unflattering description jinxed Lovell's next lunar mission. As commander of Apollo 13 (April 11–17, 1970) Lovell, with his crew-mates Fred Haise and Jack Swigert, gave the world some tense moments when an explosion aboard their spacecraft forced the three men into a dangerous and improvised return to Earth aboard the cramped and poorly equipped lunar module.

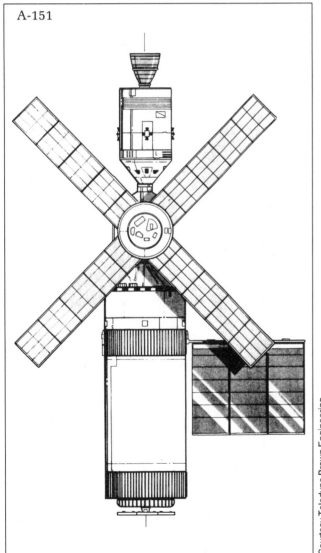

A-151

Courtesy Teledyne Brown Engineering

A top-down view of Skylab with the Apollo command module docked

A veteran of 30 days in space, in addition to his two Apollo missions Lovell had also piloted Gemini 7 (December 4–18, 1965) and Gemini 12 (November 11–15, 1966).

After retiring from NASA in March 1973 he entered private industry.

Lowell, Percival

U.S. astronomer
Born: 1855
Died: 1916

Wealthy enough to pursue his interests, Lowell was the world's most famous amateur astronomer as well as founder of the Lowell Observatory at Flagstaff, Arizona, in 1894. He was also an important force in instituting the search that led to the discovery of the planet Pluto. Lowell is most famous, however, for his "observations" of "canals" on Mars. Inspired by the writings of the Italian astronomer Giovanni Schiaparelli, Lowell believed that he was able to observe an intricate and elaborate network of artificial canals on the red planet. Not discouraged that other observers failed to report similar findings, Lowell wrote numerous articles and books in support of his observations and putting forth his theories of a dying and arid planet populated by intelligent inhabitants who dug the canals to move water from its poles to the plains. Although Lowell was mistaken in his observations, his enthusiastic writings helped to keep popular interest in astronomy and the solar system alive in the age before spacecraft.

Lucid, Shannon

U.S. astronaut
Born: January 14, 1943

Holding a B.S. in chemistry and an M.S. and Ph.D. in biochemistry, Shannon Lucid became a mission specialist for NASA in August 1979. Her first flight as mission specialist occurred aboard U.S. Space Shuttle mission 51-G (June 17–24, 1985), which deployed one scientific and three communications satellites.

Lucid made her second space flight aboard Shuttle mission STS-34, launched October 17, 1989. The crew sent the Galileo spacecraft on its way to study Jupiter, the largest planet in the Solar System and they used an instrument in the cargo bay to measure sections of the Earth's ozone layer. Ozone, whose formation is threatened by biochemical changes, forms a sort of blanket in our upper atmosphere, protecting us from most of the Sun's ultraviolet radiation. Lucid

and her crew mates landed October 23 at Edwards Air Force Base.

Lyakhov, Vladimir

Soviet cosmonaut
Born: July 20, 1941

A seasoned space traveler, Vladimir Lyakhov has spent over 362 days in space in three trouble-plagued missions. In 1988 he piloted Soyuz TM-6 to dock on August 31 with the Mir space station. Aboard he carried Abdul Ahad Mohmand, the first Afghan in space, and physician Valery Polyakov, who would remain aboard Mir with long-duration cosmonauts Vladimir Titov and Musa Manarov, who had left Earth on December 21, 1987. At the end of an uneventful week-long mission aimed primarily at public relations, however, problems began after undocking the Soyuz TM-5 return craft from Mir. With the docking module jettisoned and no possibility for return to the space station, two attempts to reenter the Earth's atmosphere aborted when the guidance system developed problems and the computer failed to allow a manual override. As oxygen and food supplies dwindled, ground control worked to adjust the programming, and the two were brought down safely in Soviet Central Asia, after 23 hours of tense anxiety, in the early morning hours of September 7. No reported fatality had occurred in the Soviet space program since the deaths of three Soyuz cosmonauts in 1971, and no one wanted to see that happen again. Lyakhov, whose capsule-side interview was carried worldwide in an unprecedented openness on the part of the Soviet Union, exhibited the supreme calm of a man who could remark blandly to ground control in the midst of the crisis, "We will endure." He was right.

During Lyakhov's first mission, Soyuz 32 (February 25, 1979) to Salyut 6, he and fellow cosmonaut Valery Ryumin spent 175 days in space without the usual monotony-breaking visits by fellow cosmonauts that most long-term Soviet space station inhabitants enjoy. Although such visits were planned, the first one was aborted, forcing the visitors to turn back, and the second was postponed altogether.

Lyakhov's second mission, the Soyuz T-9 mission to the Salyut 7 space station June 27, 1983, suffered a fuel leak, curtailing planned scientific work scheduled on the station, and then missed a major resupply visit when the resupply craft was forced to abort at launch, a circumstance that pushed the mission to its safety limits. Fortunately, Lyakhov and his fellow cosmonaut Alexandr Alexandrov managed to return safely to Earth on November 23, 1983.

M

McAuliffe, Christa

U.S. astronaut
Born: September 2, 1948
Died: January 28, 1986

Chosen from among 10,463 applicants to be the first teacher in space, McAuliffe was one of the seven space travelers killed in the Challenger disaster that occurred when an explosion destroyed U.S. Space Shuttle mission 51-L only seconds after launch on January 28, 1986.

McAuliffe had planned two lessons to give via TV to millions of schoolchildren all over the U.S.—and many of her would-be students across the country were watching that day as the Shuttle was launched from Kennedy Space Flight Center. The death of the Concord, New Hampshire, high school social studies teacher shocked the nation perhaps most deeply of all because of the eager enthusiasm she had displayed during preparations for her historic journey as the first teacher in space.

McBride, Jon

U.S. astronaut
Born: August 14, 1943

McBride, a Navy pilot, flew over 60 combat missions in Vietnam. He joined NASA in 1978, and in 1984 served as pilot for U.S. Space Shuttle mission 41-G (October 5–13, 1984).

McCandless, Bruce

U.S. astronaut
Born: June 8, 1937

McCandless, who graduated from the U.S. Naval Academy at Annapolis with a B.S. in 1958, has spent 199 hours in space. Twelve of those hours were spent in extravehicular activity (EVA). He was the first astronaut to employ the Manned Maneuvering Unit (MMU) during U.S. Space Shuttle mission 41-B (February 3–11, 1984).

Using the MMU, a strap-on personal thruster system that he helped to develop, McCandless flew untied over 300 feet away from the Shuttle.

McCulley, Michael J.

U.S. astronaut
Born: August 4, 1943

A test pilot and commander in the U.S. Navy, Michael McCulley made his first space flight as the pilot aboard Shuttle mission STS-34 (October 17–23, 1989). During the historic five-day flight the crew deployed the spacecraft Galileo, sending the highly sophisticated planetary probe on its way to explore Jupiter and its moons. They also conducted extensive photography of the Earth's ozone layer.

McCulley, who began his Naval career aboard a submarine, has flown over 50 aircraft types, logging over 4,700 flying hours, and has made nearly 400 carrier landings.

McDivitt, James

U.S. astronaut
Born: June 10, 1929

Command pilot of Gemini 4 (June 3–7, 1965), James McDivitt also commanded Apollo 9 (March 3–13, 1969), which was the first test in space of the lunar module. With David Scott in the command module, McDivitt and Rusty Schweickart moved into the lunar module, nicknamed "Spider," and ran tests in preparation for its future Moon excursions.

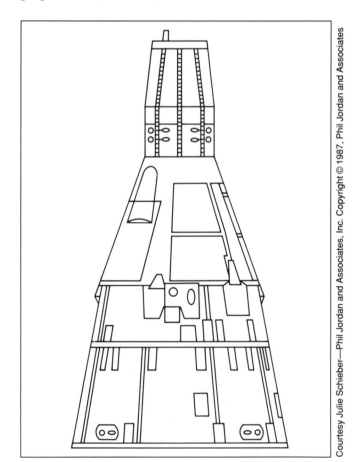

The Gemini spacecraft

An Air Force combat pilot with 145 combat missions to his credit, McDivitt has logged nearly 339 hours in space.

He retired from NASA in 1972 to enter private industry.

McKay, John

U.S. test pilot
Born: December 8, 1922
Died: April 27, 1975

One of the top U.S. test pilots during the 1950s and early 1960s, John McKay flew such advanced aircraft as the X-1 rocket plane, the Douglas Skyrocket and the X-15. After growing up in the West Indies, McKay returned to the United States and received his pilot's license at the age of 18. McKay flew combat missions for the U.S. Navy during World War II and after the war earned his B.S. in aeronautical engineering from Virginia Polytechnic Institute. Rejoining his old employer NACA (the National Advisory Committee on Aeronautics) after his graduation in 1950, he began his career as a test pilot at Edwards Air Force Base in California.

McKay flew over 20 flights on the X-15 advanced rocket plane, reaching an altitude of 295,600 feet on one of his flights on September 28, 1965. Although using Air Force standards this should have qualified him as an astronaut, McKay was not awarded astronaut wings because he was a civilian. A crash landing during one of his X-15 flights on November 9, 1962, nearly ended his life but McKay recovered to fly the plane again. His death in April 1975 was attributed to his injuries suffered in that crash.

McNair, Ronald

U.S. astronaut
Born: October 21, 1950
Died: January 28, 1986

One of the seven killed in the explosion of the Shuttle Challenger January 28, 1986, McNair was a mission specialist whose job was to have operated the Spartan scientific package during observations of Halley's Comet.

McNair had flown previously, on U.S. Shuttle mission 41-B (February 1984), when he helped to deploy two communications satellites and operated the Challenger's remote manipulator arm during the first space walks using the manned maneuvering unit (MMU).

McNair received a Ph.D. in physics from Massachusetts Institute of Technology in 1976. He did research in laser physics both at MIT and at the École

d'Étude Théorique de Physique at Les Houches, France. When he joined NASA in January 1978 he had been working as a scientist at Hughes Research Laboratories in Malibu, California, since 1976.

We have a treaty with China, don't we?
—Oleg Makarov and Vasily Lazarev, in 1975 as
their Soyuz capsule catapulted toward
the Chinese border in a crash landing

Makarov, Oleg

Soviet cosmonaut and design engineer
Born: January 6, 1933

Encouraged by the experience of his friend and fellow design-engineer Konstantin Feoktistov in Voskhod 1, engineer Oleg Makarov of Sergei Korolev's design bureau also applied to fly in space. As a result, he became one of the steady players in the Soviet program, making four flights in the position of flight engineer between 1973 and 1980.

His first flight, aboard Soyuz 12 (September 1973) with Vasily Lazarev, was the first to follow after the tragedy of Soyuz 11 during which three cosmonauts suffocated because a valve leaked during reentry. To allow enough room for three they had worn no space suits. Makarov and Lazarev wore space suits in the redesigned Soyuz and their brief two-day mission went smoothly.

Paired off again with Lazarev, Makarov was to visit Salyut 4 in a 60-day mission two years later. But luck was not with them, and their Soyuz 18-A booster aborted shortly after launch on April 5, 1975. Their command module separated from the booster and careened back to Earth, landing the two in the mountains near the Chinese border. As the Soyuz plunged downward, the cosmonauts endured an agonizing pressure of 18 Gs, which may have caused internal injuries.

Makarov, however, made it back onto the flight docket and three years later he and Vladimir Dzhanibekov took Soyuz 27 (January 1978) up to the Salyut 6 space station that Makarov had helped design. After their one-week visit with Yuri Romanenko and Georgy Grechko, who were on a 30-day long-duration mission there, they returned in Romanenko and Grechko's Soyuz 26 spacecraft, leaving the fresh vehicle at the space station.

November 1980 saw Makarov back again at Salyut 6, this time on a repair mission with fellow cosmonauts Leonid Kizim and Gennady Strekalov. After 13 days, they had the station ready for its next long-duration crew, returning aboard their Soyuz T-3 craft,

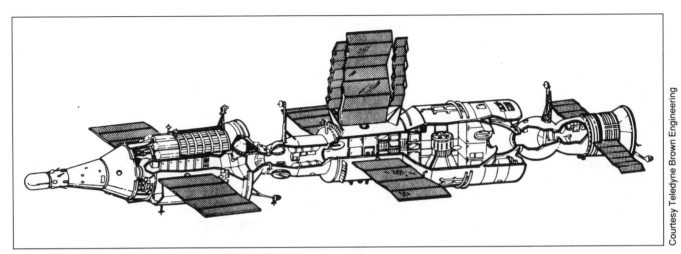

Courtesy Teledyne Brown Engineering

Mir space station docked with Cosmos 1443 (left) and Soyuz T (right)

recently redesigned to accommodate three cosmonauts again.

Speculation has it that, had the Soviets continued their lunar program, Makarov would have walked on the Moon. But even without that opportunity, he has made significant contributions as a cosmonaut and, in his current position, as senior engineer at the spacecraft bureau.

With Grigory Nemetsky, he is coauthor of *The Sails of Stellar Brigantines*, published in 1981.

Malina, Frank J.

U.S. rocket pioneer
Born: 1912
Died: 1981

Aeronautical engineer Frank Malina's pioneering work on solid-fuel rockets helped set the stage for early U.S. rocket development. With aerodynamicist Theodore von Karman, he helped found what is now NASA's Jet Propulsion Laboratory in California in the late 1930s. There, they researched high-altitude rockets, and during World War II they worked on jet-assisted takeoff (JATO) for propellor airplanes, using the same rocket principles. In 1945 von Karman and Malina tested the first WAC Corporal rocket, which they had designed for use as a high-altitude sounding rocket. It was one of the early predecessors of space-age rocket power in the U.S. Malina later left JPL to become head of the scientific research division of UNESCO in France, where he died.

Malyshev, Yuri

Soviet cosmonaut
Born: August 27, 1941

Yuri Malyshev has commanded two Soviet space flights, Soyuz T-2 (June 5, 1980) and Soyuz T-11

(April 3, 1984), during each of which he spent a week aboard the Salyut 7 space station. Staff work on the ground has since absorbed his time.

Manarov, Musa

Soviet cosmonaut
Born: 1951

As flight engineer aboard Soyuz TM-4, Musa Manarov accompanied Commander Vladimir Titov and Anatoly Levchenko to Mir on December 21, 1987, where he and Titov stayed on to begin a long-duration mission to outlast the 326-day record set in 1987 by Yuri Romanenko. The marathon one-year stay, completed December 21, 1988, was his first mission in space.

Masursky, Harold

U.S. geologist/astronomer
Born: December 23, 1922

An American geologist, Hal Masursky is a familiar figure to watchers of the American space community. Working with NASA since the U.S. Ranger series in the early 1960s, Masursky has specialized in studies of the surfaces of the Moon and planets of the Solar System and has participated in almost every NASA planetary project since that time. As leader of the team that selected and monitored observations of Mars by the Mariner spacecraft, he also helped to select the landing sites on Mars for the Viking spacecrafts, and is a member of the Venus Orbiter Imaging Radar Science Working Group. A familiar face at NASA press conferences, he has also been involved in NASA's Pioneer and Voyager projects.

Masursky is a senior scientist with the U.S. Geological Survey. He took his degree from Yale University in 1951 and has received four medals from NASA for Exceptional Scientific Achievement.

The original "Mercury 7," left to right, front row: Walter Schirra, Donald Slayton, John Glenn and Scott Carpenter. Back row, left to right: Alan Shepard, Virgil Grissom and Gordon Cooper

Soviet cosmonaut Alexei Leonov in 1974

Soviet cosmonaut Yuri Romanenko, who set a world endurance record in space aboard the Mir space station in 1987

Yuri Gagarin with his daughters, Galya and Lena, in 1963

Astronauts Tom Stafford and Eugene Cernan after recovery of Gemini 9 in June 1966

Apollo astronauts Gus Grissom (left), Ed White and Roger Chafee (right) during training in Florida. The entire crew lost their lives during a launchpad fire on January 27, 1967

NASA

The Apollo 11 crew

NASA

The crews of the joint U.S.-Soviet Apollo-Soyuz Test Project: Thomas Stafford (standing on left), commander of the American crew; cosmonaut Alexei Leonov (standing on right), commander of the Soviet crew; astronaut Donald Slayton (seated on left), docking module pilot of the American crew; astronaut Vance Brand (seated in center), command module pilot of the American crew; and cosmonaut Valery Kubasov (seated on right), engineer of the Soviet crew

French "spationauts" Patrick Baudry (left) and Jean-Loup Chrétien

U.S. Challenger Shuttle mission 51-L crew (left to right, front row) Michael J. Smith, Francis (Dick) Scobee and Ronald McNair; (rear) Ellison Onizuka, Sharon Christa McAuliffe, Gregory Jarvis and Judith Resnik. All seven died on January 26, 1986, in an explosion seconds after lift-off

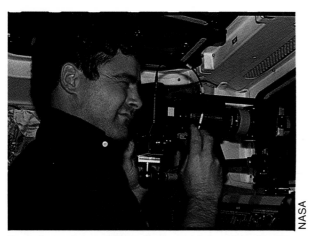

Canadian astronaut Marc Garneau during U.S. Shuttle mission 41-G in October 1984

Payload specialist Loren Acton during the Spacelab 2 mission aboard the U.S. Space Shuttle

U.S. Shuttle astronauts during the STS-7 mission in 1973. Left to right rear: Robert Crippen, crew commander; Frederick Hauck, pilot; John Fabian, mission specialist. In front, mission specialists Sally Ride and Norman Thagard

Soviet cosmonauts Leonid Popov (left), Valery Ryumin (center) and Bertalan Farkas preparing for a joint Soviet-Hungarian experiment aboard Salyut 6 in 1985

Svetlana Savitskaya at the completion of her mission aboard Soyuz T-12 in October 1984

The Fallen Astronaut/Cosmonaut: During their walk on the Moon, Apollo 15 astronauts David Scott and James Irwin left this plaque and sculpture stuck in the soil in memory of the 14 NASA astronauts and Soviet cosmonauts who had lost their lives

Five astronauts take a break from training for NASA's STS-34 mission to pose for a photo in the crew compartment trainer (CCT) in the Shuttle mockup and integration lab at Johnson Space Center. Left to right are astronauts Michael J. McCulley, pilot; Shannon W. Lucid, Franklin R. Chang-Díaz and Ellen S. Baker, all mission specialists; and Donald E. Williams, mission commander. They are wearing the orange partial pressure suits for the ascent and entry phase of flight.

It makes me proud to be a part of a country that can send a man 250,000 miles away from home, and even prouder to be a part of a country that can bring him back.

—Ken Mattingly
Apollo 16 astronaut

Mattingly, Thomas "Ken"

U.S. astronaut
Born: March 17, 1936
Ken Mattingly made his first spaceflight as command module pilot aboard Apollo 16 in April 1972. He later also commanded the U.S. Space Shuttle mission STS-4 (June 27–July 4, 1982) and Shuttle mission 51-C (January 24–27, 1985). Resigning from NASA in 1985, he became commander of the U.S. Naval Electronics Systems Command.

Merbold, Ulf

European Space Agency astronaut
Born: June 20, 1941
Born in Greiz, Germany, Ulf Merbold was the first non-American to fly into space aboard a U.S. space vehicle. A researcher at the Max-Planck Institute, Merbold was selected by the European Space Agency to be a payload specialist on U.S. Space Shuttle mission STS-9/Spacelab 1 (November 28–December 8, 1983).

Messerschmid, Ernst

German (West) astronaut
Born: May 21, 1945
Messerschmid, who received his doctorate in 1976 after studying physics at Tubingen and Bonn Universities, spent seven days aboard the U.S. Space Shuttle mission 61-A/Spacelab D-1 (October 30–November 6, 1985). Messerschmid, who has been a scientist at the CERN High Energy Physics Institute in Geneva and the Brooklyn National Laboratory in New York, was a payload specialist during the German-controlled Spacelab mission.

Mitchell, Edgar

U.S. astronaut
Born: September 17, 1930
The sixth person to walk on the Moon, Ed Mitchell was lunar module pilot of Apollo 14 (January 31–February 9, 1971). Mitchell and fellow moonwalker Alan Shepard spent over 33 hours investigating the Moon's surface.

A Navy pilot, Mitchell was one of 19 astronauts selected by NASA in April 1966. He retired from the

NASA

Astronauts Ed Mitchell (left), Alan Shepard and Stuart Roosa (right) with the Apollo 14 space vehicle

Navy and resigned from NASA in October 1972. Strongly interested in ESP (extrasensory perception) and the paranormal, Mitchell, who had attempted an ESP experiment during his Apollo flight, has founded the Institute for Noetic Studies, in Palo Alto, California. The purpose of the institute is to continue studies into ESP and similar activities. In 1974, Mitchell's coauthored book, *Psychic Exploration: A Challenge For Science*, stirred up a brief flurry of interest among ESP believers.

Mohmand, Abdul Ahad

Afghan cosmonaut
Born: 1959
The first Afghan in space, Abdul Ahad Mohmand made his Soyuz TM-6 flight to the Mir space station (docking August 31, 1988) at a time when Soviet troops were withdrawing from his country. His week-long stay was spent doing photographic surveys of Afghanistan and beaming television broadcasts of goodwill. But the trip home on Soyuz TM-5 with

Astronaut Story Musgrave

Soviet veteran Vladimir Lyakhov nearly turned public relations into disaster, when guidance problems left the two cosmonauts stranded for 23 hours orbiting in space, their food and oxygen supplies dwindling. Ground efforts to save them paid off, however, and they landed safely on September 7. Both were given awards for their courage.

Mullane, Richard

U.S. astronaut
Born: September 10, 1945
Dick Mullane has made two space flights. A mission specialist aboard U.S. Space Shuttle mission 41-D (August 30–September 5, 1984), Mullane aided in the deployment of three communications satellites and helped to erect an experimental solar- power wing. In his second space flight he served as mission specialist aboard STS-27 (December 2–6, 1988), a mission flown for the Department of Defense. Mullane is a graduate of West Point and a colonel in the U.S. Air Force.

Musgrave, Story

U.S. astronaut
Born: August 19, 1935
Serving as mission specialist aboard U.S. Space Shuttle missions STS-6 (April 4–9, 1983) and 51-F (July 19–August 6, 1985), Story Musgrave has spent over 312 hours in space, including four hours of EVA (extravehicular activity). In November 1989 he flew again, one of the first two civilian astronauts to fly aboard a military mission (STS-33, November 22–27).

A one-time high school dropout, Musgrave enlisted in the Marines in 1953. By the time he had joined NASA in 1967, as a scientist-astronaut, Musgrave had earned enough degrees for a half-dozen careers, including a B.S. in mathematics and statistics from Syracuse University (1958), an M.B.A. in operations analysis and computer programming from the University of California at Los Angeles (1959), a B.A. in chemistry from Marietta College (1960), an M.D. from Columbia University (1964) and an M.S. in physiology and biophysics from the University of Kentucky (1966). He has published over 44 scientific papers, and during his tenure at NASA he also served as part-time surgeon at Denver General Hospital and a part-time professor of physiology and biophysics at the University of Kentucky Medical Center.

N

Nagel, Steven

U.S. astronaut
Born: October 27, 1946
Steven Nagel flew as a mission specialist aboard U.S. Space Shuttle mission 51-G (June 17–24, 1985) and as pilot of mission 61-A/Spacelab D1 (October 30-November 6, 1985).

Nelson, Bill

U.S. astronaut
Born: September 29, 1942
Florida congressman Bill Nelson, the Democratic chairman of the House Space Science and Applica-tions Subcommittee, served as payload specialist on U.S. Space Shuttle mission 61-C (January 12–18, 1986). The second politician to fly in space, Nelson, like Utah senator Jake Garn, the first space-flying politician, also served as a subject for space sickness experiments.

Nelson, George

U.S. astronaut
Born: July 13, 1950
George Nelson (known as "Pinky") was chosen as one of three mission specialists for the first Shuttle mission (September 29–October 3, 1988) after the Chal-

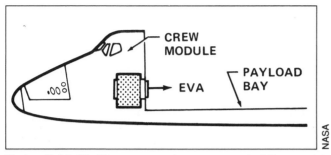

During flight, Shuttle crew members move out of the pressurized cabin quarters through an EVA airlock in order to work in the depressurized cargo or payload bay

lenger accident in January 1986. Like the other members of Discovery's five-member crew, Nelson is a Shuttle veteran—with the STS-26 mission his third Shuttle flight.

Nelson, who holds a Ph.D. in astronomy from the University of Washington, also served as mission specialist on mission 41-C (April 6–13, 1984) and mission 61-C (January 12–18, 1986).

In 1984, Nelson used the Manned Maneuvering Unit (MMU) backpack to fly out untethered to the malfunctioning Solar Maximum Satellite, trying to dock with it and haul it back aboard the Shuttle. However, he couldn't get Solar Max, as the satellite was nicknamed, to stop spinning. Ground-based engineers finally got the satellite under control, and Nelson, with fellow mission specialist James van Hoften, replaced the satellite's faulty control system module with Solar Max tilted in the Shuttle cradle. The complex process involved manipulation of dozens of tiny screws while wearing gloves that resemble boxing gloves. But Nelson and van Hoften succeeded, and they redeployed Solar Max to return to its job of collecting astronomical data.

In 1986, Nelson helped conduct experiments in astrophysics and materials processing aboard Columbia.

During the 1984 and 1986 flights alone, Nelson logged 314 hours in space, including nine hours outside the spacecraft.

Neri Vela, Rudolfo

Mexican astronaut
Born: February 19, 1952
Neri received his B.S. in mechanical and electronic engineering from the University of Mexico in 1975 and his Ph.D. in electromagnetic radiation from the University of Birmingham, England, in 1979. As a payload specialist aboard U.S. Space Shuttle mission 61-B (November 26–December 3, 1985) he conducted

four scientific experiments and aided in the launch of the Mexican Moralos B communications satellite.

Nikolayev, Andrian

Soviet cosmonaut
Born: September 5, 1929
The son of a farmer, Nikolayev attended the Marinsky-Posad Forestry Institute and worked as a lumberjack before being drafted into the Soviet army in 1950. Earning his wings as a pilot, he graduated from the Chernigov Higher Air Force School in 1954. After becoming a cosmonaut in 1960, he set an endurance record, spending four days in space aboard Vostok 3 (August 1962). As commander of the Soyuz 9 mission (June 1970), he set a new record of 18 days in space along with fellow cosmonaut Vitaly Sevastyanov.

Nikolayev, who later married the world's first woman to travel in space, Valentina Tereshkova, has written two books, *Meeting in Orbit* (1966) and *Space, A Road Without End* (1979).

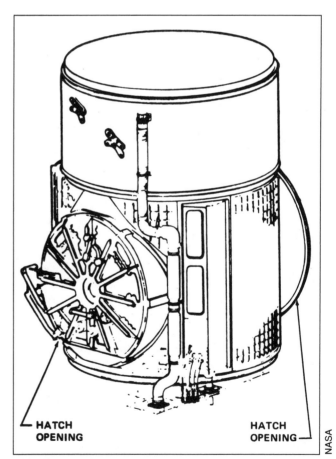

The Shuttle airlock has a pressure-sealing hatch on either side so that astronauts can exit from the crew cabin without depressurizing the cabin

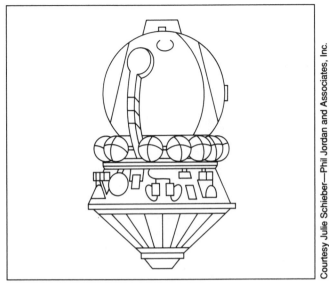

The Vostok spacecraft

Noordung, Hermann

Pseudonym of Potocnik, Austrian army captain, writer
Born: December 22, 1892
Died: August 27, 1929

Writing under the pen name "Hermann Noordung," Captain Potocnik of the Austrian reserve was a graduate engineer. Little else is known about his personal life, but his visionary writings about space, published in 1928, explored the engineering perspective of the concept of space stations in a way no one else had. He envisioned a 164-foot (50-m) wheel-shaped craft that would spin on its axis to produce artificial gravity. He has inspired many more recent concepts, including Gerard K. O'Neill's wheel-shaped "space colony." The Noordung space station also included a bowl-shaped power station and a cylinder-shaped observatory.

O

Oberth, Hermann

Hungarian mathematician, rocket pioneer
Born: June 25, 1894
Died: December 29, 1989

One of the early rocket pioneers, along with Russian Konstantin Tsiolkovsky and American Robert Goddard, Oberth never left as big a mark as had his two contemporaries. The son of a physician, he became interested in astronautics while recuperating from wounds suffered while serving in the Austro-Hungarian army during World War I. The government though wasn't interested in listening to his ideas and after the war, in 1922, his attempt to obtain his Ph.D. with a dissertation on rocket design was also rejected. Turning to his own resources, although they were greatly limited, he published a book *The Rocket into Interplanetary Space*, partly at his own expense. The book, which also included one of the first detailed discussions of orbiting space stations, was a popular success, and in 1929 he published his major work *The Road to Space Travel*.

A theorist rather than a hands-on engineer or inventor, Oberth nevertheless began to build up a following in Germany and in 1938 he joined the faculty of the Technical University of Vienna and became a German citizen. Although he worked for a while with von Braun and for the Nazis at Peenemünde, the associa-

tion was uneasy, as were his later years spent with von Braun in the United States. In 1958, after three years in the U.S., he retired and returned to Germany.

O'Connor, Bryan

U.S. astronaut
Born: September 6, 1946

Pilot of U.S. Space Shuttle mission 61-B (November 26–December 3, 1985). During the seven-day mission the crew deployed three communications satellites and experimented with space construction techniques.

Ockels, Wubbo

European Space Agency astronaut
Born: March 28, 1946

As a payload specialist aboard U.S. Space Shuttle mission 61-A/Spacelab D1, Ockels participated along with the rest of the eight-person crew in experiments in life science and materials processing designed and operated by the Federal German Aerospace Research Establishment. Ockels, who was born in the Netherlands, holds a doctorate in physics and mathematics from the University of Groningen.

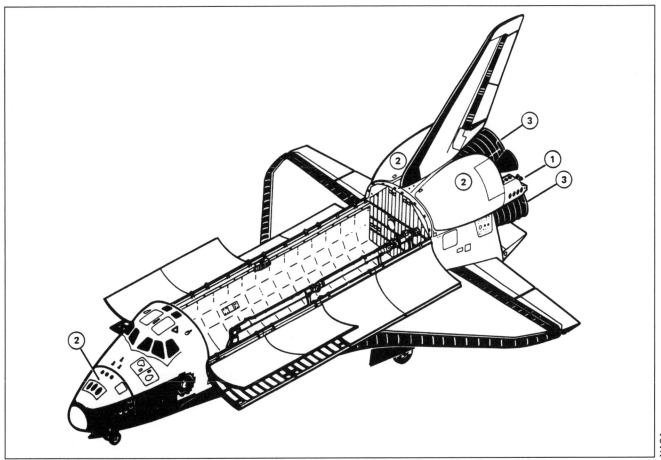

U.S. Space Shuttle with cargo bay doors open, as they are in flight, during satellite launch and retrieval maneuvers

NASA

O'Neill, Gerard

U.S. physicist
Born: February 6, 1927
A particle physicist, O'Neill graduated from Swarthmore College in 1950 and received his Ph.D. from Cornell University in 1954. Now associated with Princeton University, he is best known for his carefully designed plans for large space settlements, and his "mass-driver" (a small working model has actually been built), which would allow cheap and efficient transport of ore from the Moon's surface.

Onizuka, Ellison

U.S. astronaut
Born: June 24, 1946
Died: January 28, 1986
Ellison "El" Onizuka, the first Asian-American in space, was born June 24, 1946, in Kealakekua, Hawaii. With six other U.S. astronauts he died in the explosion of Space Shuttle Challenger on January 28, 1986.

He had made a previous flight, "classified" mission 51-C, in January 1985. During that three-day flight he helped deploy a secret U.S. Department of Defense satellite. Aboard Challenger he had planned to supervise deployment of a Tracking and Data Relay Satellite (TDRS).

Overmyer, Robert

U.S. astronaut
Born: July 14, 1936
Overmyer has logged approximately 290 hours in space as pilot of U.S. Space Shuttle mission STS-5 (November 11–16, 1982) and as commander of mission 51-B (April 29–May 6, 1985).

Holding a B.S. in physics and an M.S. in aeronautics, Overmyer worked on the design and development of the U.S. Skylab and served as a member of the support crew for the Apollo-Soyuz Test Project in 1975. Resigning from NASA in 1986 after helping in the investigation of the Shuttle Challenger disaster, he is now a private space consultant.

P

Pailes, William

U.S. astronaut
Born: June 26, 1952
William Pailes was a Department of Defense payload specialist for U.S. Space Shuttle mission 51-J (October 3–7, 1985). It is believed that the top-secret four-day mission was dedicated to the deployment of U.S. military satellites.

Stronger leadership and greater vision will be needed, but the expected benefits to America and the world will greatly outweigh the costs.
—Thomas O. Paine, chair of the National Commission on Space, on America's future commitment to space in the 21st century

Paine, Thomas

U.S. space administrator
Born: November 9, 1921
Best known in recent years as the chair of the National Commission on Space and before that as administrator of NASA from 1968 to 1970, Thomas Paine has had a strong impact on the U.S. space program.

Charged in 1985 with setting out the nation's goals in space, the Paine Commission consisted of more than a dozen space-age luminaries ranging from Nobel Prize–winning physicist Luis Alvarez to X-1 pilot Charles Yeager. The publication of their report came right on the heels of the January 1986 Challenger disaster, giving the bold visions it put forth all the more impact. They called for an ambitious agenda of exploration, development, and eventual settlement of new worlds in the next 50 years, "from the highlands of the Moon to the plains of Mars."

During the period from October 1968 to September 1970 that Paine served as acting administrator and then as NASA's third administrator, the first seven manned Apollo missions were launched. It was a time when the nation was galvanized by the excitement of seeing 21 astronauts orbit the Earth over the span of two years, with 15 of them traveling to the Moon and four of them walking on its surface.

In the mid-1980s, Paine and his commissioners found, public interest still ran high. Young people, Paine said, "were sick and tired looking at reruns. They wanted to see people walking on other worlds in real time."

Parker, Robert

U.S. astronaut
Born: December 14, 1936
As astronomer by profession, Parker was a mission specialist aboard U.S. Space Shuttle mission STS-9 (November 28–December 8, 1983). The mission was the first flight of the European-built Spacelab module.

Patsayev, Viktor

Soviet cosmonaut
Born: June 19, 1933
Died: June 30, 1971
Viktor Patsayev served as test-engineer on the ill-fated Soyuz 11/Salyut 1 mission. After an exciting 23-day mission aboard the new space station, the Soviet space program seemed to be up and running after years of frustration. But a valve in the crew's Soyuz reentry capsule leaked during descent, sucking the atmosphere out of the cabin almost instantly. Patsayev and fellow cosmonauts Georgy Dobrovolsky and Vladislav Volkov were all dead when rescuers rushed to open the spacecraft at its landing site on the Russian steppe.

Payton, Gary

U.S. astronaut
Born: June 20, 1948
Payton was a Department of Defense payload specialist aboard the U.S. Space Shuttle mission 51-C (January 24–January 27, 1985). It was later revealed that his duties included the deployment of a classified military satellite put into geosynchronous orbit for Earth observation purposes.

Pendray, G. Edward

Founder of American Rocket Society
Born: May 19, 1901
Died: September 15, 1987
A science reporter for the *New York Herald Tribune*, Pendray was one of the founders of the American Interplanetary Society (later called the American Rocket Society). He was also a fellow member of the British Interplanetary Society, elected a few months after the society was formed in 1933. After visiting Europe in 1931 and observing the work of the German Rocket Society a month after they had successfully launched their first liquid-propellant rocket, Pendray urged the AIS to follow suit. The American Interplanetary Society launched its first liquid-propellant

rocket May 14, 1933. The rocket cost a grand total of $30.60 with an additional cost of $18.80 for launch expenses. Robert Goddard, working independently, though, had already beaten the AIS to the punch and by the time of the AIS launch Goddard was already working on more advanced models of the liquid-propellant rocket.

Peterson, Donald

U.S. astronaut
Born: October 22, 1933
Mission specialist on the U.S. Space Shuttle mission STS-6 (April 4–9, 1983), Peterson joined astronaut Story Musgrave in making the first space walk of the U.S. Shuttle program.

Peterson, Forrest

X-15 pilot
Born: May 16, 1922
Forrest Peterson flew the X-15 in five flights between 1960 and 1962 to a top altitude of 101,800 feet and was the only Navy pilot to fly the experimental rocket plane. Having spent four years in the program, Peterson left in 1962 to pursue what became a highly successful career in naval aviation, during which he served as captain of the aircraft carrier USS *Enterprise*, commander of the 6th Fleet's Carrier Group Two and vice chief of naval operations for air at the Pentagon. He retired in 1980.

> *My attitude towards life is going to change, towards my family it's going to change. When I see people, I try to see them as operating human beings and try to fit myself into a human situation instead of trying to operate like a machine.*
> —Bill Pogue, on the effects of his
> Skylab experience

Pogue, William

U.S. astronaut
Born: January 23, 1930
Today a consultant to Boeing for the U.S. International Space Station, William Pogue was pilot of the longest American manned space flight to date. As part of the three-man Skylab 4 Mission (November 16, 1973–February 8, 1974) Pogue spent 84 days in space. Pogue and fellow crew members Gerald Carr and Edward Gibson gained some unwanted attention when they participated in a brief one-day "strike" in space, complaining that the ground crew's demands exceeded the time available to do their duties. The protest was brief, however, and after some com-

Bill Pogue, one of the nine astronauts who flew aboard Skylab

promises on both sides the Skylab 4 crew went on to be one of the most productive of all the Skylab missions. Skylab was Pogue's only space flight.

Polyakov, Valery

Soviet cosmonaut
Born: 1942
A physician, Valery Polyakov made his first space flight with Vladimir Lyakhov and Afghan cosmonaut Abdul Ahad Mohmand aboard Soyuz TM-6 (launched August 29, 1988). The trio docked with Mir and left Polyakov behind to keep long-duration cosmonauts Musa Manarov and Vladimir Titov under medical surveillance as they completed the second half of their mission. Manarov and Titov had arrived on Mir in December 1987 for the first year-long stay in space, which they completed December 21, 1988. Polyakov then stayed on with cosmonauts Sergei Krikalov and Alexandr Volkov, returning to Earth aboard Soyuz TM-7 after "mothballing" the space station for a period without habitation.

Popov, Leonid

Soviet cosmonaut
Born: August 31, 1945
Popov has logged over 200 days in space, including his Soyuz 35 (April 9, 1980) 185-day stay with fellow cosmonaut Valery Ryumin at the Soviet space station Salyut 6. The mission broke the record of 175 days set the previous year, also by Ryumin with Vladimir

Lyakhov. (Some record keepers maintain, however, that to break a record an increase of at least 10% must be attained, which means Soyuz 35 doesn't qualify.)

Popov has also commanded two other Soviet missions, Soyuz 40 (May 14, 1981) and Soyuz T-7 (August 19, 1982).

Popovich, Pavel
Soviet cosmonaut
Born: October 5, 1930

Pavel Popovich, the author of a biography of Yuri Gagarin, *It Couldn't Have Been Otherwise* (1980), made his only space flight aboard the Soviet spacecraft Vostok 4 (August 12–14, 1962). The mission was designed to pass within 5 miles of Vostok 3 (August 11, 1962), which had been launched the previous day.

Besides his book on Gagarin, Popovich has published an autobiography, *Takeoff in the Morning* (1974), and a book of memoirs, *Testing in Space and on Earth* (1982).

Prunariu, Dumitru
Rumanian cosmonaut-researcher
Born: September 27, 1952

Rumanian Dumitru Prunariu became the first of his countrymen to fly in space when he served as cosmonaut-researcher aboard the Soviet Soyuz 40 mission (May 1981). Prunariu and the Soyuz commander Leonid Popov spent one week of their eight-day mission linked to the Salyut 6 space station with its inhabitants Vladimir Kovalenok and Viktor Savinykh.

R

Remek, Vladimir
Czechoslovakian cosmonaut-researcher
Born: September 26, 1948

Remek served as cosmonaut-researcher aboard the Soviet mission Soyuz 28 (March 1978). Along with mission commander Alexei Gubarev he spent eight days in space, a good part of it linked up with the Soviet space station Salyut 6 and its occupants Yuri Romanenko and Georgy Grechko. Remek was the first citizen of a country other than the U.S. or Soviet Union to enter space.

Resnik, Judith
U.S. astronaut
Born: April 5, 1949
Died: January 28, 1986

An electrical engineer and classical pianist, in 1984 Judith Resnik became the second American woman to fly in space. Two years later, on her second flight, she was one of the seven-member crew killed when U.S. Space Shuttle Challenger exploded seconds after lifting off from the launchpad.

Resnik had already had a brush with death on her first flight, the maiden voyage of the orbiter Discovery. On the scheduled launch date, June 25, 1984, a main fuel valve in the third engine on the Shuttle

failed, and the computer aborted the launch. Then a fire started beneath the Shuttle's tail next to the highly explosive external tank filled with fuel. High-pressure hoses brought the fire under control and the shaken crew walked away to try again another day.

Mission 41-D did finally get off the ground on August 30, and Resnik demonstrated her skill with the remote manipulator arm, an ability she was expected to use to retrieve a Spartan satellite and bring it aboard Challenger in January 1986. She never got the chance.

Richards, Richard N.
U.S. astronaut
Born: August 24, 1946

A captain in the U.S. Navy, Dick Richards made his first space flight as pilot of the crew of U.S. Shuttle mission STS-28 (August 8–13, 1989) aboard the orbiter Atlantis. The mission's five-member crew carried payloads for the Department of Defense, along with several secondary payloads. Richards's extensive flight experience as a Naval pilot includes over 4,000 hours in 16 different types of airplanes, as well as more than 400 landings onboard various aircraft carriers. Following his STS- 28 space flight Richards has also logged five days in space.

NASA

Astronaut Sally Ride during Shuttle mission STS-7 in June 1983. A physicist, she was the first American woman to fly in space

I didn't go into the space program to make money or be famous.
—Sally Ride, in response to offers from Hollywood agents

Ride, Sally

U.S. astronaut
Born: May 26, 1951
Ride became a much-publicized space traveler when as the first American woman in space she made her historic U.S. Space Shuttle flight aboard STS-7 (June 18–24, 1983). After a second flight aboard U.S. Space Shuttle mission 41-G (October 5–13, 1984), the publicity shy Ride moved to the administrative end of NASA and was instrumental in issuing the so-called "Ride Report" in 1987, which recommended future directions and missions for the space program,

including renewed development of lunar flights, an eventual lunar base and future manned missions to Mars.

Ride retired from NASA in August 1987 to become a research fellow at Stanford University.

Romanenko, Yuri

Soviet cosmonaut
Born: August 1, 1944
One half of the Romanenko/Grechko Soyuz 26 (December 10, 1977) mission to the Soviet space station Salyut 6, Romanenko was also part of the eight-day Soyuz 38 (September 18, 1980) mission to that station and a long-duration mission to Mir in 1987.

During their 1977–1978 stay aboard Salyut 6, Romanenko and Grechko gained international fame by staying in space for a then record-breaking 96 days. The mission has sometimes been referred to as "the flight of the classics," since "Grechko" and "Romanenko" are Ukrainian for *Greek* and *Roman.*

Romanenko's most recent success was in 1987, when he set yet another record—326 days aboard the Mir space station. The previous record had been 237 days, set by Leonid Kizim, Vladimir Solovyov and Oleg Atkov aboard Salyut 7 in 1984. During Romanenko's marathon he performed several extravehicular activities (EVAs) with fellow cosmonaut Alexander Laveikin, one to clear the docking area for a 27-ton astrophysical module, and two to erect a third solar panel for the space station.

Roosa, Stuart

U.S. astronaut
Born: August 16, 1933
The "third man on the totem pole," Roosa was the command module pilot of Apollo 14 (January 31–February 9, 1971). Holding his post in the "Kitty Hawk," Roosa orbited the Moon while fellow astronauts Alan Shepard and Edgar Mitchell spent 33 hours on the lunar surface. Roosa has logged nearly nine days in space. Retiring as an Air Force colonel, he resigned from NASA in 1976 to enter the private sector.

Ross, Jerry

U.S. astronaut
Born: January 20, 1948
Jerry Ross, a lieutenant colonel in the U.S. Air Force, has flown in space as a mission specialist aboard two

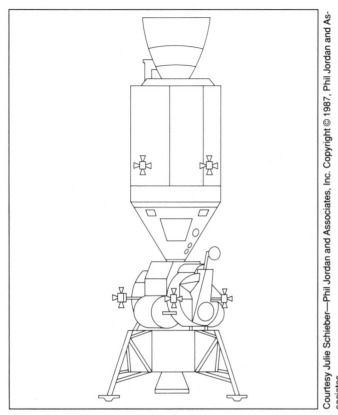

The Apollo spacecraft: Command/Service Module (CSM) and Lunar Module (LM)

Space Shuttle missions, STS 61-B (November 26–December 3, 1985) and STS-27 (December 2–6, 1988).

Mission 61-B was a highly eventful flight, carrying the heaviest payload ever flown by the Shuttle. During the mission Ross helped demonstrate that construction (such as would be necessary in building the planned Space Station Freedom) is possible in space. He and fellow astronaut Sherwood Spring made two six-hour space walks during which they wielded huge demonstration trusses and secured them in place to show how structures might be built by workers in the weightlessness of space. Numerous other experiments were also run during the flight, including several for the Mexican government.

STS-27 was a slightly shorter mission of only four days, flown for the Department of Defense. It was the second flight (the first of the orbiter Atlantis) flown following the 1986 Challenger disaster.

Rozhdestvensky, Valery

Soviet cosmonaut
Born: February 13, 1939
Rozhdestvensky's only space mission, Soyuz 23 (October 1976), almost ended in disaster.

Rozhdestvensky and his fellow cosmonaut commander Vyacheslav Zudov had been scheduled for a month-long stay aboard the Soviet space station Salyut 5 when their spacecraft's guidance system failed. The link-up was called off and the mission hastily aborted, forcing Rozhdestvensky and Zudov to make an unscheduled night spashdown in the middle of a snowstorm over Lake Tengiz in the Soviet Union. Although rescue workers were able to reach the bobbing spacecraft, they couldn't pull it ashore until morning, forcing Rozhdestvensky and Zudov to spend an anxious and dangerously cold night aboard.

Rukavishnikov, Nikolai

Soviet cosmonaut
Born: September 18, 1932
Soviet cosmonaut Nikolai Rukavishnikov's Soyuz 16 mission (December 2, 1974) was a successful Soviet dress rehearsal for their upcoming participation in the Apollo/Soyuz rendezvous.

Rukavishnikov's two other missions had both involved failures. As a part of the Soyuz 10 mission (April 23, 1971) he was scheduled to take part in occupying and operating the world's first space station, Salyut 1, but the mission was returned to Earth, without the cosmonauts having boarded the station, when technical problems arose.

Rukavishnikov's later mission, Soyuz 33 to the Salyut 6 space station (April 10, 1979) with cosmonaut Georgy Ivanov, was aborted en route due to engine failure.

Rushworth, Robert

X-15 pilot
Born: October 9, 1924
Bob Rushworth made more flights in the X-15 rocket plane than any other pilot. During one of his 34 flights, on June 27, 1963, he reached an altitude of 55 miles or 285,000 feet, earning astronaut status by the Air Force definition. Over the course of his career he flew 50 different aircraft, logging more than 6,500 hours of flying time.

Rushworth started out in 1943 as a U.S. Army enlisted man. He trained as an aviation cadet and became a pilot in 1944, after which he flew combat missions in China, Burma and India. He left the military in 1946 to get a degree in mechanical engineering. But by February 1951 he was back in the Air Force, earned an M.S. in aeronautical engineering in 1954 and became a test pilot. From 1957 to 1966 he flew experimental aircraft and rocket planes at Ed-

Cosmonauts Valery Ryumin (right) and Vladimir Lyakhov relax, playing chess during training

TASS from SOVFOTO

wards Air Force Base, earning a Distinguished Flying Cross for a tricky landing of the X-15.

In 1966 he went back into combat duty, this time in Vietnam. On returning to the States in 1969, he served as commander of several test centers. He is now retired.

If it was needed to prove we could go to Mars, then Leonid [Popov] and I would volunteer right now.

—Valery Ryumin

Ryumin, Valery

Soviet cosmonaut
Born: August 16, 1939
The first man to travel 150 million miles, Valery Ryumin, a long-duration specialist, held the record for total logged time in space—361 days, 21 hours and 34 minutes—until he was topped in 1986. What's unusual is that his record actually happened by accident.

On his first flight, Soyuz 25, Ryumin and commander Vladimir Kovalenok were to open up the new Salyut 6 space station for a planned 90-day stay, but they ran into docking problems and had to return just two days later.

Reassigned to another crew, on February 25, 1979, Ryumin traveled with Vladimir Lyakhov to Salyut 6 aboard Soyuz 32. They spent a record 175 days in space and, although a little lonely when planned visits from other crews didn't work out, they returned in good spirits and good health. They had no plans to return soon.

Ryumin went to work training Leonid Popov and Valentin Lebedev, the next crew slated to travel to Salyut 6. But when Lebedev broke his knee on a trampoline, Ryumin volunteered to fill in. That's how Leonid and Ryumin happened to break Ryumin's own record about a year later, launching aboard Soyuz 35 on April 9, 1980, and returning on October 11. Opening a letter he had left aboard the space station in 1979 for the crew to follow, Ryumin muttered wryly, "I am not in the habit of writing letters to myself."

63

S

Sagan, Carl

U.S. astronomer
Born: November 9, 1934

One of the best-known astronomers in America, Sagan has done much in his many popular television appearances to put astronomy and the space program before the American people. Sagan received his Ph.D. at the University of Chicago in 1960 and in 1968 became associate professor of astronomy and director for planetary studies at Cornell University. Although Sagan's primary interests are planetary surfaces and atmospheres, an area in which he has done much respected scientific work, he has also done pioneering studies in the possibilities of extraterrestrial life in the universe. A vocal and untiring advocate of science, Sagan is the author of many popular books, including two outside the field of astronomy, *The Dragons of Eden* and *Broca's Brain*.

Sagdeyev, Roald

Soviet scientist
Born: 1933

As head of Russia's Institute for Space Research (IKI) Sagdeyev is credited with breathing new life into the Soviet space program in the early 1970s. Under Sagdeyev's direction the program not only became more open but realized such spectacular successes as the Venera 9 and 10 projects to Venus and the Vega mission to Halley's Comet.

Sarafanov, Gennady

Soviet cosmonaut
Born: January 1, 1942

Sarafanov flew aboard Soyuz 15 (August 26, 1974), but the mission was aborted before its planned arrival at Salyut 3. Sarafanov and fellow cosmonaut Lev Demin were forced to return to Earth.

Soviet cosmonaut Svetlana Savitskaya (left) with fellow Soyuz T-7 crew members Leonid Popov and Alexandr Serebrov (right)

TASS from SOVFOTO

al-Saud, Sultan Bin Salman

Saudi Arabian astronaut
Born: June 27, 1956

The first Arab to go into space, Prince Sultan Bin Salman al-Saud spent a week as civilian payload specialist aboard the U.S. Space Shuttle Discovery during Mission 51-G (June 17–24, 1985). Al Saud, who was acting director of the Saudi Arabian television commercial department at the time of his flight, relayed televised broadcasts describing the Shuttle mission back to his country. After his Shuttle flight, the prince joined the Saudi air force as a pilot, holding the rank of major.

> *When I was a child in school, my geography teachers would hammer into my mind the names of the different countries on the Earth and the outlines of the boundaries between them ... But as I looked down from orbit, I saw no such lines or marks. Before the end of our mission all of us in the crew agreed that from space we saw only one planet, only one Earth.*
> —Sultan Bin Salman al-Saud

Savinykh, Viktor

Soviet cosmonaut
Born: March 7, 1940

Viktor Savinykh has logged more than 250 days in space on three space flights: Soyuz T-4 (March 12 to May 26, 1981) to Salyut 6 with Vladimir Kovalenok, during which they were visited by both a Mongolian and a Rumanian cosmonaut; Soyuz T-13 (June 6 to September 26, 1985), with Vladimir Dzhanibekov, his partner in an exciting rescue of Salyut 7; and Soyuz TM-5 (June 7–17 1988) to Mir, with Anatoliy Solovyov and Bulgarian cosmonaut Alexandr Alexandrov.

Savitskaya, Svetlana

Soviet cosmonaut
Born: August 8, 1948

The second Soviet woman to fly in space, Savitskaya and fellow cosmonauts Leonid Popov and Alexandr Serebrov, flew the Soyuz T-7 mission (August 19, 1982) to link up with the Soviet space station Salyut 7. During her second flight aboard a Soyuz spacecraft, the Soyuz T-12 (July 17, 1984), she became the second woman in space, performing 3½ hours of extravehicular activity (EVA).

Levity is appropriate in a dangerous trade.
—Walter Schirra

Schirra, Walter

U.S. astronaut
Born: March 12, 1923

A veteran of the U.S. Apollo program, Walter "Wally" Schirra has flown Mercury, Gemini and Apollo spacecraft.

As pilot of the Mercury-Atlas 8 (October 3, 1962) during the early days of the American space program, Schirra's six-orbit, 9 hour and 13 minute space flight helped pave the way for the next U.S. step into space, the Gemini program. On the two-man Gemini-Titan 6-A mission (December 15–16, 1965), Schirra and Thomas Stafford added a lighthearted note by reporting to have sighted a UFO resembling Santa Claus and then concluding their report with Schirra giving an off-key rendition of "Jingle Bells."

The Apollo 7 mission (October 11–22, 1968) was conducted in a more serious vein. In the course of 11 days in space, Schirra and his fellow astronauts Donn Eisele and Walter Cunningham had the unenviable job of proving the controversial Apollo spacecraft qualified for flight after the tragic launchpad fire that killed Gus Grissom, Roger Chaffee and Edward White on January 27, 1967.

Today Schirra is a businessman and occasional television pitchman.

Schmitt, Harrison

U.S. astronaut
Born: July 3, 1935

The first scientist to walk on the moon, Harrison Schmitt flew on the Apollo 17 (December 7–19, 1972) lunar landing mission. The mission was the last of the Apollo series. Schmitt, a geologist, spent three days on the lunar surface with fellow astronaut Eugene Cernan while command module pilot Ronald Evans orbited above. The mission, which made extensive use of the Lunar Rover, was one of the most scientifically successful of the Apollo series.

Schmitt resigned from NASA in 1975, and in 1976 was elected to the U.S. Senate from the state of New Mexico. He is currently a private consultant.

Schweickart, Russell

U.S. astronaut
Born: October 25, 1935

Russell "Rusty" Schweickart logged 241 hours in space during the flight of Apollo 9 (March 3–13,

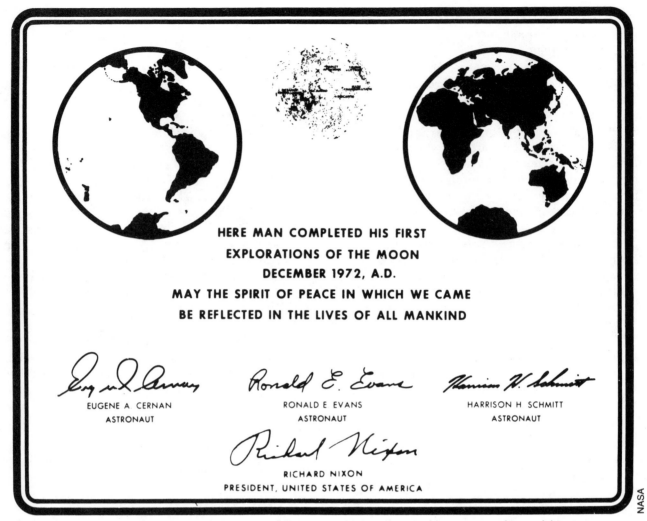

HERE MAN COMPLETED HIS FIRST
EXPLORATIONS OF THE MOON
DECEMBER 1972, A.D.
MAY THE SPIRIT OF PEACE IN WHICH WE CAME
BE REFLECTED IN THE LIVES OF ALL MANKIND

EUGENE A. CERNAN
ASTRONAUT

RONALD E EVANS
ASTRONAUT

HARRISON H. SCHMITT
ASTRONAUT

RICHARD NIXON
PRESIDENT, UNITED STATES OF AMERICA

NASA

Apollo 17 astronauts Eugene Cernan and Harrison Schmitt left this plaque on the Moon to greet future visitors

1969). Schweickart, along with his fellow astronauts James McDivitt and David Scott, flew in Earth orbit to test the Apollo lunar module and pressure suits in preparation for later Apollo lunar landings.

Scobee, Francis

U.S. astronaut
Born: May 19, 1939
Died: January 28, 1986

Along with all six members of his crew, Commander Dick Scobee was killed when Shuttle flight 51-L exploded seconds after lift-off on January 28, 1986. The mission would have deployed a TDRS-B communications satellite; it was scheduled to perform observations of Halley's Comet with the Spartan satellite; and Christa McAuliffe, the first "teacher in space," was going to give lessons televised from the spacecraft to thousands of schoolchildren. The tragedy brought all U.S. manned space operations to a halt while inves-

tigations, redesign and testing took place. The halt lasted more than 2½ years.

Scobee came to 51-L after serving as pilot on Shuttle mission 41-C in April 1984. The crew of that mission succeeded in capturing, repairing and redeploying the Solar Maximum satellite, saving $187 million. The mission also released an 8,000-pound platform of scientific experiments called the Long Duration Exposure Facility (LDEF). Scheduled for retrieval by Challenger, the LDEF was left stranded in space, destroying or modifying many of the experiments.

Scobee spent a total of seven days in space.

Scott, David

U.S. astronaut
Born: June 6, 1932

Alongside pilot Neil Armstrong, Scott participated in the Gemini 8 (March 16, 1966) practice space docking with an unmanned Agena spacecraft. Later, as com-

NASA

Physician Rhea Seddon "sits" down to a meal on the mid deck during U.S. Shuttle mission 51-D

mand module pilot for Apollo 9 (May 3–13, 1969), he piloted the spacecraft, nicknamed "Gumball," while fellow astronauts James McDivitt and Russell Schweickart made a free flight test in Earth orbit of the lunar module, nicknamed "Spider."

Getting a chance to do some testing on the "ground," Scott joined fellow moonwalker James Irwin in the Apollo 15 (July 26–Aug 7, 1971) test of the Lunar Rover as the two put the snappy little four-wheel drive electric car through its paces on the Moon's surface.

During his three missions, Scott has logged over 545 hours in space, 20 hours and 46 minutes of it in extravehicular activity (EVA).

Scully-Power, Paul

U.S. astronaut
Born: May 28, 1944
A professional oceanographer, Paul Scully-Power had an opportunity to practice his profession from a new vantage point when he made ocean observations from aboard U.S. Space Shuttle mission 41-G (October 5–13, 1984). Previously he had been an earthbound assistant for astronauts doing oceanic observations aboard the Skylab flights. Although 41-G was Scully-Powers's only flight, he is a seasoned professional who has made over 24 scientific oceanic cruises.

Australian by birth, and educated in Australia and London, England, Scully-Power has published over 60 scientific papers.

Seddon, Rhea

U.S. astronaut
Born: November 8, 1947
Rhea Seddon logged 148 hours in space as a member of U.S. Space Shuttle mission 51-D (April 12–19, 1985). Her duties included launching a Navy communications satellite, which, although successfully deployed, failed to activate and was picked up and repaired by a later mission.

Serebrov, Alexandr

Soviet cosmonaut
Born: February 14, 1944
Serebrov, who has become something of a world spokesman for the Soviet space program, has flown thus far on two Soviet missions—Soyuz T-7 (August 19, 1982), which included Svetlana Savitskaya, the second woman in space, and the Soyuz T-8 mission (April 20, 1983), which was aborted before completion.

Sevastyanov, Vitaly

Soviet cosmonaut
Born: July 8, 1935
Vitaly Sevastyanov has flown two Soviet missions, Soyuz 9 (June 1, 1970) and Soyuz 18 (May 24, 1975). He has spent over 81 days in space.

Sharma, Rakesh

Indian cosmonaut-researcher
Born: January 13, 1949
Rakesh Sharma spent eight days aboard Soyuz T-11 (April 1984). As a cosmonaut-researcher he shared duties with cosmonauts Yuri Malyshev and Gennady Strekalov as Soyuz linked up with the Soviet space station Salyut 7 and its crew: Leonid Kizim, Vladimir Solovyov and Oleg Atkov.

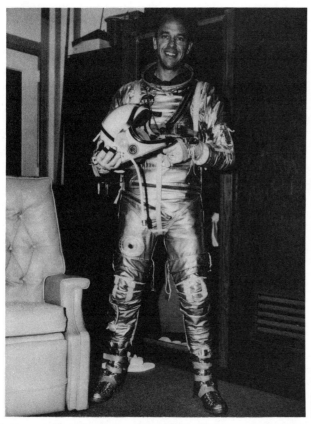

Astronaut Alan Shepard suited up in the Mercury pressure suit

NASA

Shatalov, Vladimir

Soviet cosmonaut
Born: December 8, 1927
Shatalov has flown on three Soviet missions, Soyuz 4 (January 14, 1969), Soyuz 8 (October 13, 1969) and the Soyuz 10 (April 23, 1971) mission to the Salyut 1 space station. Although his third mission was intended to be a record-breaking stay aboard the space station, the crew could not open the hatch between the two vehicles and the mission had to be called back after only five hours.

Shaw, Brewster

U.S. astronaut
Born: May 16, 1945
Logging a total of 534 hours in space during three flights, Brewster Shaw made his first space flight as the pilot of the U.S. Space Shuttle STS-9/Spacelab 1 (November 28–December 8, 1983) and was commander of U.S. Space Shuttle mission 61-B (November 26–December 3, 1985) as well as STS-28 (August 8–13, 1989).

A colonel in the U.S. Air Force, Shaw has received numerous medals and awards, including the NASA

Special Achievement Award and the NASA Outstanding Leadership Medal (both in 1988). He served as a member of the Rogers Presidential Commission investigating the STS 51-L Challenger accident and also headed a group responsible for implementing safety standards before return to flight on the Shuttle orbiter following the 1986 accident. Also a liaison between NASA and the Department of Defense, his most recent flight, STS-28, carried DoD payloads. He is now deputy director of shuttle operations at Kennedy Space Center.

Why don't you fix your little problem ... and light this candle?
—Alan Shepard, eager to get on with the countdown on his Mercury flight

Shepard, Alan

U.S. astronaut
Born: November 18, 1923
On May 5, 1961, Alan Shepard became the first American in space when he took a 15½ minute suborbital flight for 304 miles (489km), reaching an altitude of 116 miles before landing in the Pacific. The flight was short and sweet and effective. America had its first man in space. Shepard later recounted that the flight happened so fast that he only managed a 30-second glimpse out of the spacecraft's small window. Shepard managed to get a better view of space 10 years later, though, when as commander of Apollo 14 (January 31–February 9, 1971) he spent two days on the surface of the Moon.

The only one of the original seven Mercury astronauts to fly to the Moon, Shepard was born in East Derry, New Hampshire, the son of a career Army officer. Although his father had attended West Point, Shepard earned his B.S. from the United States Naval Academy in 1944. After service in World War II he attended the U.S. Navy Test Pilot School at Patuxent River in 1950, later serving as an instructor from 1951 to 1953.

After retiring from NASA and the Navy in 1974, Shepard entered the private sector. In 1971 he served as a delegate to the 26th United Nations General Assembly.

Shepherd, William

U.S. astronaut
Born: July 26, 1949
A graduate of the U.S. Naval Academy and a captain in the U.S. Navy, William Shepherd made his first space flight as mission specialist aboard the orbiter

Atlantis Space Shuttle mission STS-27 (December 2–6, 1988). He and his four crew mates carried a payload for the Department of Defense in addition to several other payloads. Shepherd holds degrees of Ocean Engineer and a masters of science in mechanical Engineering from the Massachusetts Institute of Technology.

Shonin, Georgy

Soviet cosmonaut
Born: August 3, 1935
Georgy Shonin commanded the Soyuz 6 (October 11, 1969) mission, on which cosmonaut Valery Kubasov became the first human to practice construction techniques in space.

He has written an account of the first group of Soviet cosmonauts, *The Very First*, published in 1977.

Shriver, Loren

U.S. astronaut
Born: September 23, 1944
As pilot of the U.S. Space Shuttle mission 51-C (January 24–27, 1985), the first Department of Defense mission, Shriver logged just over three days in space.

I would give my left arm to be the first man in space.

—Deke Slayton

Slayton, Donald "Deke"

U.S. astronaut
Born: March 1, 1924
One of the original Mercury Seven astronauts selected in 1959, Deke Slayton was grounded by a heart problem and didn't have a chance to fly until his ASTP (Apollo-Soyuz Test Project) flight, July 15–24, 1975. During that well-publicized flight, a joint mission and link-up in space between the U.S. and Soviet Union, Slayton and his fellow astronauts Thomas Stafford and Vance Brand docked with a Soviet Soyuz spacecraft and spent two days sharing quarters and conducting experiments with Russian Cosmonauts Alexei Leonov and Valery Kubasov. Slayton almost gave more than his left arm when, after unlinking and spending five more days in space alone, the Apollo spacecraft accidentally filled with deadly exhaust gas on its return splashdown. Slayton's lungs were severely burned and the three-man Apollo crew came near to losing their lives.

In a final irony for Slayton, a small tumor unrelated to the accident was discovered on one of his lungs and he was again temporarily grounded.

Astronaut Donald "Deke" Slayton in the hatchway between the Apollo Docking Module and the Soyuz Orbital Module as the two docked spacecraft orbit the Earth during the joint U.S.-Soviet Apollo-Soyuz Test Project

Apollo-Soyuz was Slayton's only space flight, but during it he logged a total of nearly nine days in space.

Retiring from NASA in 1981, he joined the private sector.

Smith, Michael

U.S. astronaut
Born: April 30, 1945
Died: January 28, 1986
Michael Smith piloted Shuttle mission 51-L, which exploded seconds after lift-off on January 28, 1986, killing all seven crew members. It was his first mission in space, although he was an experienced aircraft pilot with more than 4,500 hours of flying time, 4,200 hours on jets.

Solovyov, Anatoliy

Soviet cosmonaut
Born: 1948
A new pilot-cosmonaut on the scene in 1988, Anatoliy Solovyov made his first flight aboard Soyuz

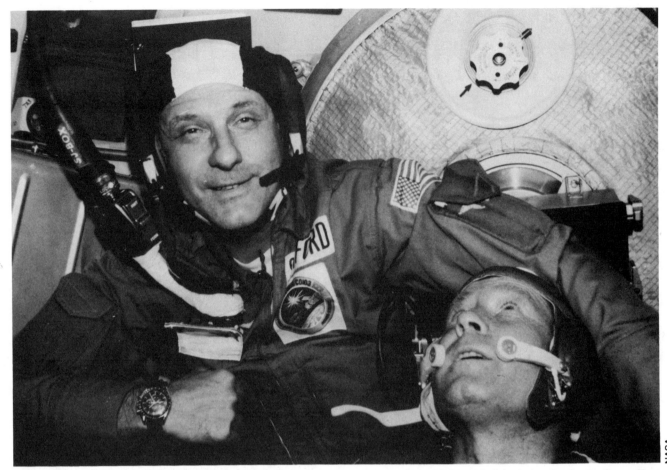

NASA

U.S. astronaut Tom Stafford (left) with Soviet cosmonaut Alexei Leonov in the Soyuz Orbital Module during the Apollo-Soyuz Test Project

TM-5, with Viktor Savinykh and Bulgarian cosmonaut Alexandr Alexandrov. Launched June 7, 1988, they visited Musa Manarov and Vladimir Titov aboard the space station Mir, returning to Earth in the long-duration cosmonauts' Soyuz TM-4 spacecraft.

Solovyov, Vladimir

Soviet cosmonaut
Born: November 11, 1946

A seasoned space veteran, Vladimir Solovyov has made two visits to space. In 1984 he was flight engineer aboard Soyuz T-10 and spent 237 days in space on Salyut 7—a record not broken until 1987. With him were commander Leonid Kizim and Oleg Atkov, a cardiologist. In addition to participating in many experiments to judge the effects of weightlessness on human beings after long exposure, Solovyov performed more than 20 hours of extravehicular activity (EVA) repairing the Salyut 7 main rocket engines.

For Solovyov's second mission he teamed once again with Kizim, this time to open up the new Mir space station in 1986. Arriving at Mir in mid-March, three weeks after its launch, Kizim and Solovyov activated the station. Then on May 5, they took their Soyuz T-15 spacecraft to dock with Salyut 7, where they demonstrated girder construction techniques during two space walks and picked up experiments left behind by the last crew. They headed back to Mir on June 25 and returned to Earth on July 16 after mothballing the station to wait for its next crew.

By the end of the two missions, Solovyov had spent nearly 352 days in space, with 31 hours of EVA to his credit.

Spring, Sherwood

U.S. astronaut
Born: September 3, 1944

As a mission specialist on U.S. Space Shuttle mission 61-B (November 26–December 3, 1985), Sherwood "Woody" Spring took part in the first extravehicular space construction test. Spring and fellow astronaut Jerry Ross assembled and disassembled prototypes of future space station elements in an attempt to demonstrate that such space construction was feasible. Of Spring's 165 hours of logged space time, 12 hours and 14 minutes were spent outside the spacecraft.

Springer, Robert

U.S. astronaut
Born: May 21, 1942
Robert Springer's first space flight, as mission specialist aboard U.S. Space Shuttle mission STS-29 (March 13–18, 1989), was an especially successful flight. Springer and his crew mates deployed a TDRS (Tracking and Data Relay Satellite), performed a "heat pipe" radiator experiment testing technology to be used on the Space Station Freedom and completed several other experiments including a protein crystal growth experiment and a chromosome and plant cell division experiment. They also took over 3,000 photographs of the Earth using several types of cameras.

With 119 hours in space logged after his first flight, Springer also flew 550 combat missions in Vietnam and has logged more than 3,800 hours flying time in aircraft, including 3,300 hours in jet aircraft.

Stafford, Thomas

U.S. astronaut
Born: September 17, 1930
The soft-spoken Stafford, nicknamed "Mumbles" by his fellow astronauts, made four space flights between 1965 and 1975. His missions included copiloting Gemini 6-A (December 15–16, 1965) with Walter Schirra; commanding Gemini 9-A (June 3–6, 1966) with Eugene Cernan; commanding Apollo 10 (May 18–26, 1969) with Cernan and John Young; and commanding the American participants in the ASTP (Apollo/Soyuz) linkup mission (July 15–24, 1975). He logged over 21 days in space.

Stafford, who has also coauthored training manuals for test pilots, retired from NASA in 1975 to become a private businessman.

Stewart, Robert

U.S. astronaut
Born: August 13, 1942
"Bob" Stewart has made two flights aboard the U.S. Space Shuttle. During the first—mission 41-B (February 3–11, 1984)—he participated in testing the Manned Maneuvering Unit, a thruster-propelled backpack that allows astronauts to fly outside the Shuttle untethered. Stewart's second mission was

51-J (October 3–7, 1985), when as a mission specialist he participated in the deployment of two Department of Defense satellites. Stewart has logged 289 hours in space, 12 of those spent in extravehicular activity.

Strekalov, Gennady

Soviet cosmonaut
Born: October 28, 1940
Out of flight engineer Gennady Strekalov's four space missions, two have succeeded and two have failed.

On his first (November 27–December 10, 1980), with Oleg Makarov and Leonid Kizim, he tested the new Soyuz T-model accommodations for a crew of three. The Soyuz T-3 mission was the first time three cosmonauts had flown together since 1971. They docked with Salyut 6, performed some repairs and returned home.

Strekalov's second mission was to be an eight-month marathon, with Vladimir Titov and Alexandr Serebrov, aboard Salyut 7. But shortly after their April 20, 1983, launch, the cosmonauts realized that their Soyuz T-8 could not dock with the space station because the rendezvous radar wasn't working.

Five months later, Strekalov and Vladimir Titov were set for another visit to Salyut 7, this time to visit cosmonauts Lyakhov and Alexandrov. But a fire broke out on the launchpad. To rescue the two cosmonauts, the escape rocket was ignited in a launchpad abort, pulling the Soyuz T-10 capsule away from danger, popping up a few thousand feet and parachuting it safely to the ground.

After the Soyuz T-8 and T-10-1 frustrations, Strekalov had a turn of luck. When Nikolai Rukavishnikov fell ill in March 1984, Strekalov stepped in as flight engineer on Soyuz T-11. The seven-day mission to Salyut 7 took place in April with Yuri Malyshev and Indian cosmonaut Rakesh Sharma aboard.

I love it.

—Kathryn D. Sullivan,
the first American woman to walk in space

Sullivan, Kathryn

U.S. astronaut
Born: October 3, 1951
The first U.S. woman to walk in space, Sullivan spent 3½ hours in extravehicular activity (EVA) during her flight aboard U.S. Space Shuttle mission 41-G (October 5–13, 1984). Outside the Challenger orbiter, she and David Leestma tested the ability of space workers to perform in zero gravity, successfully installing a valve assembly into simulated satellite propulsion

plumbing, a job that would be required for in-orbit refueling of Landsat satellites.

Thus far, Sullivan, who holds a Ph.D. in geology, has logged approximately 198 hours in space. She was co-investigator for the Shuttle Imaging Radar system flown during her mission aboard Challenger, and she has also pursued her career in geoscience by flying aboard NASA's high-altitude WB-57F aircraft. She is adjunct professor of geology at Rice University.

Houston, we've got a problem here.
—Jack Swigert from Apollo 13, just after explosion in oxygen tank

Swigert, John
U.S. astronaut
Born: August 30, 1931
Died: December 27, 1982
As command module pilot for the nearly disastrous

Apollo 13 mission (April 11-17, 1970), John Swigert shared one of the most harrowing three-day space rides in the history of the American space program.

The problem began when an oxygen tank in the spacecraft exploded, aborting the mission to the moon but leaving the crew no way to turn back. Swigert and his crew mates, James Lovell and Fred Haise, were forced to circumnavigate the Moon under extremely hazardous conditions. A second oxygen tank damaged by the explosion began leaking. Conditions in the service module portion of the spacecraft deteriorated rapidly, and when all power in the damaged module was lost the three men were forced into the cramped lunar module for their tense ride home.

It was Swigert's only space flight. Retiring from NASA in 1973, he entered politics. Swigert died of bone cancer on December 27, 1982, in Washington, D.C. His death came only a week before he was to be sworn in as a U.S. congressman from Colorado.

T

Tamayo-Mendez, Arnaldo
Cuban cosmonaut-researcher
Born: January 29, 1942
Tamayo-Mendez was a cosmonaut-researcher aboard Soyuz 38 (September 1980). With fellow cosmonaut Yuri Romanenko, he spent eight days in space, seven of them linked with the Soviet Salyut 6 space station and cosmonauts Leonid Popov and Valery Ryumin. Tamayo-Mendez was the first black and Hispanic to fly in space.

If you're afraid of the wolves, don't go in the woods.
—Valentina Tereshkova, when asked if she was afraid during her Vostok mission

Tereshkova, Valentina
Soviet cosmonaut
Born: March 6, 1937
The first woman to fly in space, Valentina Tereshkova faced her mission with very little training and considerable courage. On June 16, 1963, her tiny Vostok 6 capsule was lifted into orbit to the great roar of its boosters. There she spent three days circling the

Earth, completing 48 orbits. In one mission she outshone all six American Project Mercury astronauts who had flown up to that time, and her call sign "Chaika" ("Seagull") caught the imaginations of women everywhere whose vision extended beyond traditional homemaking and motherhood. She made television broadcasts from space and kept in constant radio contact with Valery Bykovsky, who was flying Vostok 5 at the same time.

The American space program, by contrast, did not put a woman in space until June 18, 1983, a decision that brought criticism and charges of sexism to the program. But Tereshkova, it turns out, was an accomplished parachutist, especially fit for the rigors of early space travel. And, ironically, the Soviets have included only one other woman in their space program, Svetlana Savitskaya, in 1982 and 1984, with no plans for including any others.

Thagard, Norman
U.S. astronaut
Born: July 3, 1943
Originally trained as a physician, Thagard has logged over 17 days in space. He has served as a mission

specialist aboard the U.S. Space Shuttle STS-7 (June 18–24, 1983), aboard Spacelab 3 (April 29–May 6, 1985); and on STS-30 (May 4–8, 1989).

During STS-7, which was the second flight for the orbiter Challenger and the first with its crew increased to five, the crew deployed satellites for Canada (ANIK C-2) and Indonesia (PALAPA B-1) and completed several exercises in preparation for future satellite retrieval and repair missions. Thagard collected data on the physiological effects of space on humans and operated the Canadian-built Remote Manipulator System (a huge robotic arm for changing the orientation of satellites and other objects in space).

On the STS 51-B/Spacelab-3 science mission Thagard assisted the commander and pilot on ascent and entry, helped deploy the NUSAT satellite, and cared for the 24 rats and two squirrel monkeys carried onboard for the study of physiological effects of microgravity.

STS-30 was a four-day mission aboard the orbiter Atlantis, during which the crew deployed the Magellan planetary spacecraft for its mission to the planet Venus. With completion of his third flight, Thagard has logged a total of more than 17 days in space.

Soviet cosmonaut Valentina Tereshkova, the first woman in space, with fellow cosmonauts Yuri Gagarin (left), the first man in space, and Alexei Leonov, the first spacewalker

Thompson, Milton

X-15 pilot
Born: May 4, 1926

NASA test pilot Milton Thompson flew various experimental craft, including the X-15 (14 times). He was scheduled to fly the Dyna-Soar X-20 plane, but it never got off the drawing boards. He did, however, pioneer flight of a wingless "lifting body" aircraft in 1963 that was a distant precursor of the Space Shuttle.

Thornton, Kathryn

U.S. astronaut
Born: August 17, 1952

The first woman to fly on a military space mission, Thornton made her historic flight aboard Shuttle flight STS-33 in November 1989. She was also one of the first two non-military astronauts to fly a dedicated Department of Defense mission. (Story Musgrave, who flew aboard the same mission, was the other.)

Thornton received a Ph.D. in physics from the University of Virginia in 1979 and participated in numerous nuclear physics research programs, including those at Oak Ridge National Laboratory and Brookhaven National Laboratory. She received a NATO postdoctoral fellowship to continue her research at the Max Planck Institute for Nuclear Physics in Germany and was employed as a physicist by the U.S. Army from 1980 to 1984, when she was selected by NASA to become an astronaut.

Thornton, William

U.S. astronaut
Born: April 14, 1929

At 54 years of age, William Thornton was the oldest U.S. citizen to fly in space at the time of his first space flight aboard the U.S. Space Shuttle mission STS-8 (August 30–September 5, 1983). He later served aboard mission 51-B/Spacelab 3 (April 29–May 6, 1985).

Tikhomirov, N. I.

Russian Rocket Pioneer
Born: 1860
Died: 1930

As early as 1894, N. I. Tikhomirov had begun experiments that would become the first practical research in Russian rocketry. By 1912 he had presented his plans for development of a liquid-propellant rocket to the minister of the Russian navy, and he continued to submit proposals over the coming years. The uneasy political climate following the Russian Revolution left his work all but unnoticed, until finally, in 1919, he caught the attention of officials, having made a direct appeal to Lenin in May of that year. Two years later, the Revolutionary Military Council set up a research laboratory for the study of rocket propulsion. With his assistant, V. A. Artemiev, Tikhomirov's lab officially opened on March 1, 1921, in Moscow. The lab concentrated on solid-rocket propellants and performed tests between 1923 and 1925, moving to Leningrad in 1925. By 1928, Tikhomirov's laboratory had become the GDL (Gas Dynamics Laboratory), with an official affiliation with the Soviet Military Research Council. The work of the GDL that ensued became the foundation from which today's Russian rocketry was to develop. Much of it had begun with the work of its founder, N. I. Tikhomirov.

Tikhonravov, Mikhail K.

Russian rocket pioneer
Born: 1900
Died: 1974

Designer of the first hybrid, solid/liquid propellant rocket, Mikhail Tikhonravov saw his concept take off in a successful test rocket, GIRD 09, on August 17, 1933. The rocket was built by a team that included Sergei Korolev, who was to become unquestionably the greatest figure in Soviet rocket design. During its test, GIRD 09 reached a height of 1,312 ft (400 m), and the event was recorded with fervor: "... starting with this moment Soviet rockets must fly over the Union of Republics ... Soviet rockets must conquer space!"

Titov, Gherman

Soviet cosmonaut
Born: September 11, 1935

Titov's sole space flight aboard Vostok 2 (August 6, 1961) was the second orbital flight to be performed by a human. Titov spent 24 hours orbiting the Earth, a then record-breaking 17 times.

Titov, Vladimir

Soviet cosmonaut
Born: January 1, 1947

Vladimir Titov, a distant relative of fellow cosmonaut Gherman Titov, had the misfortune to fly two failed Soviet missions. A third was more successful.

As commander of Soyuz T-8 (April 20, 1983), a planned eight-month mission to the Salyut 7 space station, he and fellow cosmonauts Gennady Strekalov and Alexandr Serebrov were forced to abandon the rendezvous when a radar failure made docking too difficult. Titov had another stroke of bad luck when he and Strekalov were preparing to be launched (Sep-

tember 1983) as a relief crew to Salyut 7. Fire broke out at the base of the launch vehicle, forcing the ground crew to separate their module by escape rockets, and Titov and Strekalov landed three miles from the launchpad, shaken up but unhurt.

More recently, however, Titov flew aboard Soyuz TM-4 with Musa Manarov to begin a long-duration mission aboard the Mir space station in December 1987. During their historic year-long stay they entertained numerous visitors, including a Bulgarian and an Afghan cosmonaut.

Toftoy, Holger N.

U.S. military officer
Born: October 31, 1902
Died: April 19, 1967

As U.S. chief of technical intelligence for army ordnance in Europe, Toftoy was responsible for "Operation Paperclip," which brought Wernher von Braun and approximately 129 other German scientists and engineers to the United States after World War II.

Known as "Mr. Missile," Toftoy was continuously instrumental in the early development of guided mis-

Soviet cosmonaut Gherman Titov, the second man to orbit the Earth, receives congratulations after his Vostok 2 flight in 1961

siles including the Redstone missile, which was one of the pioneering rockets used in the U.S. space program. He served for four years as commanding general of Redstone Arsenal in Huntsville, Alabama (1954-1958) prior to his retirement in 1960.

Truly, Richard

U.S. astronaut
Born: November 12, 1937
Truly has logged over eight days in space during his two U.S. Space Shuttle missions, STS-2 (November 12–14, 1981) and STS-8 (August 30–September 5, 1983). STS-8 was the first U.S. Space Shuttle mission to be launched and to land at night. Truly succeeded James Fletcher (in his second term) as administrator of NASA in April 1989, after serving as associate administrator for space transportation systems since February 1986.

Tsander, Fridrikh

Russian space pioneer
Born: 1887
Died: 1933
Among Russia's foremost early rocket pioneers, Fridrikh Arturovitch Tsander began working on liquid-propelled rocket engines in the 1920s. Static tests of his rockets—the OR-1 powered by gasoline and air and the OR-2 propelled by gasoline and oxygen—had begun by the 1930s. He also pioneered the idea of a space station, along with several of his contemporaries, including K. E. Tsiolkovsky and Y. V. Kondratyuk, Hermann Oberth, Walter Hohmann, Guido von Pirquet and Hermann Noordung. Tsander's book, *Problems of Flight by Means of Reactive Devices* (or, problems of jet propulsion), published in 1932, made a significant contribution in that field. In November 1933, the same year Tsander died, the first Soviet fully liquid-propellant rocket, GIRD X, was successfully tested. It was powered by Tsander's OR-2 engine.

The earth is the cradle of mankind, but mankind cannot stay in the cradle forever.
—K. I. Tsiolkovsky

Tsiolkovsky, Konstantin

Russian pioneer space theorist
Born: September 17, 1857
Died: September 19, 1935
Sometimes called "the grandfather of the space age," Konstantin Tsiolkovsky is seen by many as the prophet of today's modern space programs, both Soviet and American. Born to a poor Russian family, Tsiolkovsky was a self-educated schoolteacher who had been practically deaf from childhood. Taking an early interest in the problems of space and space flight, he wrote a remarkable series of technical papers and articles dealing with all aspects of his subject from astronautics to space suits and colonization of the solar system, including the problems of building and operating future space stations.

"The Earth is the cradle of mankind, but mankind cannot stay in the cradle forever," Tsiolkovsky once wrote. In a fitting tribute the inscription on his gravesite reads "Mankind will not remain tied to the Earth forever."

Well-informed opinion is that the Soviet government planned to launch their first artificial satellite, Sputnik, on the hundredth anniversary of Tsiolkovsky's birth, but delays slipped the launch by several days.

Tuan, Pham

Vietnamese cosmonaut-researcher
Born: February 14, 1947
The first Asian in space, Vietnamese Pham Tuan served as cosmonaut-researcher, with fellow cosmonaut Viktor Gorbatko, aboard the Soviet Soyuz 37 (July 1980), spending eight days in space as Soyuz linked up with the Salyut space station and its occupants Leonid Popov and Valery Ryumin.

SOVFOTO

Russian rocket pioneer Konstantin Tsiolkovsky

V

Van Allen, James

U.S. physicist
Born: September 7, 1914
A tireless advocate for space science and an occasional opponent of NASA's manned space program, James van Allen was born in Mount Pleasant, Iowa, and received his Ph.D. in 1939 from the University of Iowa. Van Allen's early research was devoted to the field of cosmic radiation. In 1958 his research led to the discovery of the "Van Allen belts" by NASA's Explorer 1 satellite. The belts, Van Allen concluded after exacting investigation, were intense zones of high radiation caused by trapped charged particles.

van den Berg, Lodewijk

U.S. astronaut
Born: March 24, 1932
As payload specialist aboard the U.S. Space Shuttle mission 51-B/Spacelab 3 (April 29–May 6, 1985), van den Berg participated in experiments in space medicine and manufacturing.

Van Hoften, James

U.S. astronaut
Born: June 11, 1944
Van Hoften has flown on two U.S. Space Shuttle missions, 41-C (April 6–13, 1984) and 51-I (August 27–September 3, 1985), during which he logged nearly 14 days in space, including 22 hours of extravehicular activity (EVA). Nicknamed "Ox" because of his size, at 6 feet 4 inches and over 210 pounds, Van Hoften is one of the largest of the American astronauts.

Vasyutin, Vladimir

Soviet cosmonaut
Born: March 8, 1952
Vasyutin was commander of the Soyuz T-14 mission to Salyut 7 (September 17, 1985). The mission plans called for Vasyutin and fellow cosmonauts Georgy Grechko and Alexandr Volkov to spend an extended stay aboard the space station during which time they would make observations of Halley's Comet in March of 1986. Vasyutin became seriously ill with an infection, however, and the cosmonauts were forced to return in late November 1985 after only 65 days in space. It was the unfortunate Vasyutin's only space mission.

Verne, Jules

French writer
Born: 1828
Died: 1905
Although not as popular with science-fiction readers today as in the past, the writings of Jules Verne have captured the minds and imaginations of generations of readers. His tales, ranging from space voyages to undersea journeys, have inspired such space-age pioneers as Konstantin Tsiolkovsky and Wernher von Braun, and such science-fiction writers as H. G. Wells and Ray Bradbury. His indelible character Captain Nemo of *Twenty Thousand Leagues Under the Sea* (1870) remains a fictional prototype of mythic proportions even today, and Verne's unerring sense of wonder and adventure can still delight and enchant.

Viktorenko, Alexander

Soviet cosmonaut
Born: 1946
Rookie pilot Alexander Viktorenko made his first trip into space as commander of Soyuz TM-3, launched July 22, 1987, and headed for the Mir space station. With him were Muhammed Faris, a Syrian cosmonaut, also on his first flight, and Alexandr Alexandrov, who would stay to take the place of the ailing long-duration cosmonaut Alexander Laveikin. After a brief stay Viktorenko returned to Earth with Faris and Laveikin aboard.

Volk, Igor

Soviet cosmonaut
Born: April 12, 1937
Igor Volk has spent 12 days in space as a flight engineer aboard the Soviet Soyuz T-12 mission to the space station Salyut 7 (July 17, 1984).

Volkov, Alexandr

Soviet cosmonaut
Born: May 27, 1948
Alexandr Volkov served as cosmonaut-researcher aboard the Soyuz T-14 mission to Salyut 7 (September 17, 1985). The planned mission was cut short, however, when commander Vladimir Vasyutin became ill, and the crew was forced to return to Earth 65 days into the mission.

Volkov flew a second mission, this time as commander, with Sergei Krikalov and Jean-Loup Chrétien of France, aboard Soyuz TM-7 (launched November 26, 1988). Volkov performed a space walk with Chrétien during the visit at the Mir space station where long-duration cosmonauts Vladimir Titov and Musa Manarov were completing a year-long stay. He returned with Krikalov and Polyakov April 27, 1989, leaving Mir uninhabited.

You look down there and you get homesick. You want some sunshine, fresh air, you want to wander in the woods.

—Vladislav Volkov

Volkov, Vladislav

Soviet cosmonaut
Born: November 23, 1935
Died: June 30, 1971
Volkov was flight engineer aboard the ill-fated Soyuz 11 flight that met initially with enormous success, including an unprecedented 23-day stay aboard a space station. Headed for home, as the crew jettisoned the docking module a pressure equalization valve blew open prematurely. Volkov and fellow cos-

monauts Georgy Dobrovolksy and Viktor Patsayev were not wearing pressurized suits and all three died instantly.

Volynov, Boris

Soviet cosmonaut
Born: December 18, 1934
As commander of Soyuz 5, Boris Volynov participated in the first docking of two manned spacecraft. The other craft, Soyuz 4, was piloted by Vladimir Shatalov. Once docked, Volynov's passengers, fellow cosmonauts Yevgeny Khrunov and Alexei Yeliseyev, put on space suits. They emerged from Soyuz 5, pulled themselves over toward Soyuz 4 and climbed aboard, returning to Earth with Shatalov and leaving Volynov to return alone.

In July to August 1976 Volynov also commanded the Soyuz 21 mission to Salyut 5 with engineer Lt. Col. Vitaly M. Zholobov. A problem developed with Salyut's atmosphere, however, and the crew returned to Earth after only 49 days, three weeks earlier than planned.

W

Walker, Charles

U.S. astronaut
Born: August 29, 1948
As a civilian payload specialist Walker has served on three U.S. Space Shuttle missions, 41-D (August 30–September 5, 1984), 51-D (April 12–10, 1985) and 61-B (November 26–December 3, 1985). He has logged over 458 hours in space.

Walker, David

U.S. astronaut
Born: May 20, 1944
Pilot of U.S. Space Shuttle mission 51-A (November 8–16, 1984), David Walker logged nearly eight days on his first flight in space. During the mission the crew deployed two satellites and, in the first space salvage mission in history, retrieved the Palapa B-2 and Westar VI satellites for return to Earth.

In May 1989 Walker commanded Shuttle mission STS-30, during which the crew of five deployed the

planetary spacecraft Magellan from the cargo bay of the orbiter Atlantis. Headed for an encounter with the planet Venus in mid-1990, Magellan will use specialized radar instruments to map the entire surface of the planet. With completion of the four-day flight (May 4–8, 1989), Walker has logged a total of 12 days in space.

Walker, Joseph

U.S. test pilot
Born: February 20, 1921
Died: June 8, 1966
Between March 1960 and August 1963, Joe Walker made 25 flights in the X-15 experimental rocket plane at Edwards Air Force Base. He set world records in both speed and altitude, taking the feisty plane to 4,104 miles per hour and to an altitude, on August 22, 1963, of almost 67 miles (354,300 feet). Walker made two X-15 flights to altitudes higher than 62 miles, which is the International Aeronautical Federation (FAI) standard for qualifying space flights. Joe Walker

died in a mid-air crash on June 8, 1966. He was flying an F-104 Starfighter.

Wang, Taylor

U.S. astronaut
Born: June 16, 1940

As a payload specialist aboard U.S. Space Shuttle mission 51-B/Spacelab 3 (April 29–May 6, 1985), Taylor Wang conducted an experiment that he had designed specifically for the mission—to test the dynamics of space manufacturing. Born in Shanghai, China, Wang was raised in Taiwan. He later moved with his family to America, where he received his B.S., M.S. and Ph.D. degrees in physics at the University of California at Los Angeles. Wang became an American citizen in 1971.

Webb, James E.

U.S. space administrator
Born: October 7, 1906

James E. Webb became NASA's second administrator in February 1961 and served until October 1968. During his tenure, the Mercury, Gemini and Apollo programs were developed.

Wells, Herbert George

British Writer
Born: 1866
Died: 1946

Although Herbert George Wells, better known as H. G., was an accomplished author of social commentary, essayist and historian, he is best known today for his science-fiction novels, most notably *The Time Machine* (1895), *The Invisible Man* (1897) and *The War of the Worlds* (1898). An astute observer of science and technology, Wells had an inventive mind that was one of the most admired and controversial of his time, and his works are still as fresh and readable today as they were when first written.

Weitz, Paul

U.S. astronaut
Born: July 25, 1932

As the pilot of Skylab SL-2 (May 25–June 22, 1973), the first manned visit to America's first space laboratory, Paul Weitz, along with his fellow crew members Charles Conrad and Joseph Kerwin, spent 28 days in space. He added another five days of space

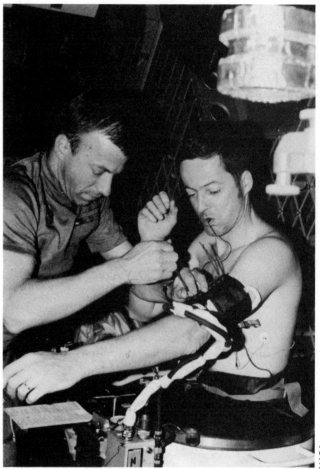

Skylab 2 pilot Paul Weitz (left) assists scientist-astronaut Joe Kerwin with a blood pressure cuff during an in-flight experiment to test the human cardiovascular system's adaptation to weightlessness

time to his log when he commanded U.S. Space Shuttle flight STS-6 (April 4–9, 1983). STS-6 was the first flight of the ill-fated Challenger Space Shuttle, which was later to explode at launch on January 28, 1986.

Weitz is currently Deputy Director of the Johnson Space Center in Houston, Texas.

White, Alvin

X-15 pilot
Born: December 9, 1918

Like Scott Crossfield, Al White was a test pilot employed by North American Aviation, the company that developed the X-15. He was Crossfield's backup and went through the same training, but never got to fly the X-15, although he flew many flights aboard chase planes.

X-15 test pilot Robert White receives congratulations from Col. Charles Yeager (left), the first man to fly faster than the speed of sound

White, Edward

U.S. astronaut
Born: November 14, 1930
Died: January 27, 1967

Gemini 4 astronaut Ed White became the first American to walk in space on June 3, 1965. Attached to his spacecraft by a long tether, White floated out into the vast vacuum of space while fellow crew member James McDivitt took some of the most stunning photographs of the space program. White tested a small gas handgun used to propel himself for part of his 10-minute extravehicular activity (EVA), giving better control than just pushing off could do. The two returned to Earth after four days in orbit.

With Gus Grissom and Roger Chaffee, White was scheduled to make the first flight in the Apollo series that would ultimately land human beings on the Moon. But as the three sat sealed and strapped inside

the Apollo 1 cabin during a dry-run test, a sudden spark from an electrical short resulted in an instant inferno, raging through the pure-oxygen atmosphere. Grissom, Chaffee and White never had a chance to get out.

White was buried at West Point.

White, Robert

X-15 pilot
Born: July 6, 1924

The first person to fly a plane to an altitude higher than 50 miles, X-15 pilot Robert White qualified for Air Force astronaut wings on July 17, 1962, reaching an altitude of 314,750 feet, more than 59 miles. He didn't, however, meet the test of "flying in space," later established by the Fédération Aeronautique Internationale (FAI) at 62 miles (100 km). In November

1961 he also became the first to fly at Mach 6, six times the speed of sound.

Williams, Donald
U.S. astronaut
Born: February 13, 1942
Williams was the pilot of the 16th U.S. Space Shuttle mission, 51-D (April 12–19, 1985). It was the fourth flight of the orbiter Discovery. The crew deployed two satellites, ANIK-C for Telesat of Canada and Syncom IV-3 for the U.S. Navy. For the first time, because of malfunctions of the Syncom satellite, the 51-D crew had to perform an unscheduled EVA (extravehicular activity, or space walk), along with unplanned proximity and rendezvous operations, to repair the satellite. They landed at Kennedy Space Center.

Williams made use of his experience when he went on to become commander of the orbiter Atlantis on mission STS-34, launched October 17, 1989. During this historic mission—long awaited by planetary scientists—the crew sent the spacecraft Galileo on its way to study the planet Jupiter and its moons. They also studied the ozone layer in Earth's upper atmosphere. STS-34 came to successful completion on October 23, landing at Edwards Air Force Base in California.

Worden, Alfred
U.S. astronaut
Born: February 7, 1932
As command module pilot of Apollo 15 (July 26–August 7, 1971) Worden "held the fort" orbiting the Moon for three days while his fellow crew members, David Scott and James Irwin visited the lunar surface. It was Worden's only space flight.

Retiring from the U.S. Air Force and resigning from NASA in 1975, he later published a children's book, *A Flight to the Moon* (1974), and a book of poetry, *Hello, Earth: Greetings from Endeavor* (1974). Worden is a businessman today.

Y-Z

Yegorov, Boris
Soviet cosmonaut
Born: November 26, 1937
Boris Yegorov made a one-day flight aboard the Soviet Voskhod 1 mission (October 12, 1964). The first physician to fly in space he observed the effects of weightlessness on fellow cosmonauts Vladimir Komarov and Konstantin Feoktistov.

Yeliseyev, Alexei
Soviet cosmonaut
Born: July 13, 1943
Alexei Yeliseyev was one of the two cosmonauts who emerged from Soyuz 5, after it docked with Soyuz 4 in January 1969. Protected by their space suits, Yeliseyev and Yevgeny Khrunov floated hand over hand to Soyuz 4, where they joined Vladimir Shatalov and returned home aboard his craft. The mission simulated some aspects of space rescue and it was the second space walk in the Soviet program.

October of that same year saw Yeliseyev in space again, this time for six days aboard Soyuz 8, one of three Soviet spacecraft in orbit at the same time.

Disappointment came, however, in April 1971 when a planned 30-day mission (Soyuz 10) was aborted. Yeliseyev, with Shatalov and Nikolai Rukavishnikov, headed for the new Salyut space station on April 23. But although they docked successfully, they couldn't enter the space station. Frustrated, they returned to Earth on April 25.

It was Yeliseyev's third mission in a three-year period for a total of nine days in space and one hour of extravehicular activity.

> *The dream is alive again.*
> —John Young, Commander, STS-1,
> the successful first Shuttle flight

Young, John
U.S. astronaut
Born: September 24, 1930
As a veteran of six space flights Young has logged over 835 hours in space. His first mission was as pilot for Gemini 3 (March 23, 1965) when with fellow astronaut Gus Grissom he tested the first manned spacecraft to maneuver in orbit. Young's second space mission was Gemini 10 (July 18–21, 1966), during which he served as commander with pilot Michael Collins. The Gemini missions had been in preparation for America's Apollo Moon series, and in May 1969 Young served as command module pilot for Apollo

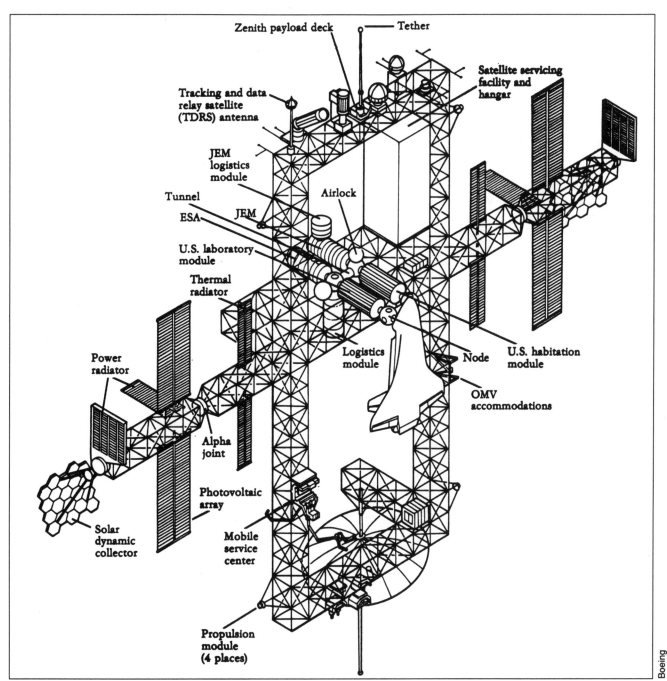

Tether

Zenith payload deck

Satellite servicing facility and hangar

Tracking and data relay satellite (TDRS) antenna

JEM logistics module

Airlock

Tunnel

ESA

JEM

U.S. laboratory module

Thermal radiator

Logistics module

Node

U.S. habitation module

OMV accommodations

Power radiator

Alpha joint

Photovoltaic array

Solar dynamic collector

Mobile service center

Propulsion module (4 places)

Boeing

Design proposal for U.S./International Space Station Freedom, where astronauts will work in Earth orbit year-round

10 (May 18–26, 1969), a mission that took its crew of Young and fellow astronauts Thomas Stafford and Eugene Cernan into lunar orbit. With Young waiting aboard the command module, Stafford and Cernan approached to within 10 miles of the lunar surface but the mission was only an elaborate dress rehearsal for a lunar landing and no touchdown on the Moon was made. Young finally made it to the Moon, though, when as commander of Apollo 16 (April 16–27, 1972) he and fellow astronaut Charles Duke spent 3 days on

the lunar surface while command module pilot Thomas Mattingly orbited overhead.

Moving over to the U.S. Space Shuttle program, Young's next command was aboard America's first Space Shuttle flight STS-1 (April 12–14, 1981), with Robert Crippen as pilot.

His last space flight to date was Shuttle mission STS-9 (November 28–Dec 8, 1983), the first flight to carry the European-built Spacelab. Young had also been scheduled to command the Shuttle launch of the

Hubble Space Telescope in 1986 when the Challenger tragedy forced a postponement of the mission.

Zholobov, Vitaly

Soviet cosmonaut
Born: June 18, 1937
With commander Boris Volynov, flight engineer Vitaly Zholobov was scheduled to spend a 60-day stay aboard Salyut 5 when Soyuz 21 was launched on July 6, 1976. While much of their work involved military surveillance, they also studied the effects of weightlessness on plants and animals. But possible psychological problems and troubles with the air purification system aboard Salyut brought an early end to their stay after only 49 days. They returned on August 24, 1976.

Zudov, Vyacheslav

Soviet cosmonaut
Born: January 8, 1942

Vyacheslav Zudov holds the distinction of commanding the only Soviet mission ever to make a splashdown, instead of a soft landing on hard ground. Zudov and flight engineer Valery Rozhdestvensky lifted off aboard Soyuz 23 on October 14, 1976, and headed for the Salyut 5 space station, where they planned to stay for at least 60 days. But on arrival they discovered they couldn't dock and had to make an emergency return to Earth. It was late at night in the middle of a blizzard and they landed in Lake Tengiz, a salt-water lake located within the designated Soviet landing area.

APPENDIX
MEN AND WOMEN IN SPACE—SOVIET MISSIONS

Mission	Cosmonaut(s)	Launch Date
Vostok 1	Gagarin	April 12, 1961
Vostok 2	G. Titov	Aug. 6–7, 1961
Vostok 3	Nikolayev	Aug. 11–15, 1962
Vostok 4	Popovich	Aug. 12–15, 1962
Vostok 5	Bykovsky	June 14–19, 1963
Vostok 6	Tereshkova	June 16–19, 1963
Voskhod 1	Komarov, Yegorov, Feoktistov	Oct. 12–13, 1964
Voskhod 2	Belyayev, Leonov	March 18–19, 1965
Soyuz 1	Komarov (died on reentry)	April 23–24, 1967
Soyuz 3	Beregovoy	Oct. 26–30, 1968
Soyuz 4	Shatalov	Jan. 14–17, 1969
Soyuz 5	Volynov, Yeliseyev, Khrunov	Jan. 15–18, 1969
Soyuz 6	Shonin, Kubasov	Oct. 11–16, 1969
Soyuz 7	Filipchenko, V. Volkov, Gorbatko	Oct. 12–17, 1969
Soyuz 8	Shatalov, Yeliseyev	Oct. 13–18, 1969
Soyuz 9	Nikolayev, Sevastyanov	June 1–19, 1970
Soyuz 10	Shatalov, Yeliseyev, Rukavishnikov	April 23–25, 1971
Soyuz 11	Dobrovolsky, V. Volkov, Patsayev (crew died during reentry)	June 6–30, 1971
Soyuz 12	Lazarev, Makarov	Sept. 27–29, 1973
Soyuz 13	Klimuk, Lebedev	Dec. 18–26, 1973
Soyuz 14	Popovich, Artyukhin	July 3–19, 1974
Soyuz 15	Sarafanov, Demin	Aug. 26–28, 1974
Soyuz 16	Filipchenko, Rukavishnikov	Dec. 2–8, 1974
Soyuz 17	Gubarev, Grechko	Jan. 11–Feb. 9, 1975
Soyuz 18-A	Lazarvev, Makarov (failed launch)	April 5, 1975
Soyuz 18	Klimuk, Sevastyanov	May 24–July 26, 1975
Soyuz 19	Leonov, Kubasov (Apollo-Soyuz Test Project)	July 15–21, 1975
Soyuz 21	Volynov, Zholobov	July 6–Aug. 24, 1976
Soyuz 22	Bykovsky, Askenov	Sept. 15–23, 1976
Soyuz 23	Zudov, Rozhdestvensky	Oct. 14–16, 1976
Soyuz 24	Gorbatko, Glazkov	Feb. 7–25, 1977
Soyuz 25	Kovalenok, Ryumin	Oct. 9–11, 1977
Soyuz 26	Romanenko, Grechko	Dec. 10–Mar. 16, 1977

Mission	Cosmonaut(s)	Launch Date
Soyuz 27	Dzhanibekov, Makarov	Jan. 10–16, 1978
Soyuz 28	Gubarev, Remek (Czechoslovakia)	March 2–10, 1978
Soyuz 29	Kovalenok, Ivanchenkov	June 15–Nov. 2, 1978
Soyuz 30	Klimuk, Hermaszewski (Poland)	June 27–July 5, 1978
Soyuz 31	Bykovsky, Jaehn (German Democratic Republic)	Aug. 26–Sept. 3, 1978
Soyuz 32	Lyakhov, Ryumin	Feb. 25–Aug. 19, 1979
Soyuz 33	Rukavishnikov, Ivanov (Bulgaria)	April 10–12, 1979
Soyuz 35	Popov, Ryumin	April 9–Oct. 11, 1980
Soyuz 36	Kubasov, Farkas (Hungary)	May 26–June 3, 1980
Soyuz T-2	Malyshev, Aksenov	June 5–9, 1980
Soyuz 37	Gorbatko, Tuan (Vietnam)	July 23–31, 1980
Soyuz 38	Romanenko, Tamayo-Mendez (Cuba)	Sept. 18–26, 1980
Soyuz T-3	Kizim, Makarov, Strekalov	Nov. 27–Dec. 10, 1980
Soyuz T-4	Kovalenok, Savinykh	March 12–May 26, 1981
Soyuz 39	Dzhanibekov, Gurrugcha (Mongolia)	March 22–30, 1981
Soyuz 40	Popov, Prunariu (Romania)	May 14–22, 1981
Soyuz T-5	Berezovoy, Lebedev	May 13–Dec. 10, 1982
Soyuz T-6	Dzhanibekov, Ivanchenkov, Chrétien (France)	June 24–July 2, 1982
Soyuz T-7	Popov, Serebrov, Savitskaya	Aug. 19–27, 1982
Soyuz T-8	V. Titov, Strekalov, Serebrov	April 20–22, 1983
Soyuz T-9	Lyakhov, Alexandrov	June 27–Nov. 23, 1983
Soyuz T-10-1	Titov, Strekalov (launchpad abort)	Sept. 26, 1983
Soyuz T-10	Kizim, V. Solovyov, Atkov	Feb. 8–Oct. 2, 1984
Soyuz T-11	Malyshev, Strekalov, Sharma (India)	April 3–11, 1984
Soyuz T-12	Dzhanibekov, Savitskaya, Volk	July 17–29, 1984
Soyuz T-13	Dzhanibekov, Savinykh	June 6–Sept. 26, 1985
Soyuz T-14	Vasyutin, Grechko, A. Volkov	Sept. 17–Nov. 21, 1985
Soyuz T-15	Kizim, V. Solovyov	March 13–July 16, 1986
Soyuz TM-2	Romanenko, Laveikin	Feb. 5–Dec. 28, 1987
Soyuz TM-3	Viktorenko, Alexandrov (USSR), Faris (Syria)	July 22–30, 1987
Soyuz TM-4	Levchenko, Titov, Manarov	Dec. 21, 1987–Dec. 21, 1988
Soyuz TM-5	A. Solovyov, Savinykh, Alexandrov (Bulgaria)	June 7–15, 1988
Soyuz TM-6	Lyakhov, Polyakov, Mohmand (Afghanistan)	Aug. 29–Sept. 7, 1988
Soyuz TM-7	A. Volkov, Krikalov, Chrétien (France)	Nov. 26–Dec. 21, 1988

MEN AND WOMEN IN SPACE—U.S.

MISSIONS

Mission	Astronaut(s)	Dates
Mercury-Redstone 3	Shepard	May 5, 1961
Mercury-Redstone 4	Grissom	July 21, 1961
Mercury-Atlas 6	Glenn	Feb. 20, 1962
Mercury-Atlas 7	Carpenter	May 24, 1962
Mercury-Atlas 8	Schirra	Oct. 3, 1962
Mercury-Atlas 9	Cooper	May 15–16, 1963
Gemini-Titan 3	Grissom, Young	Mar. 23, 1965
Gemini-Titan 4	McDivitt, White	June 3–7, 1965
Gemini-Titan 5	Cooper, Conrad	Aug. 21–29, 1965
Gemini-Titan 7	Borman, Lovell	Dec. 4–18, 1965
Gemini-Titan 6-A	Schirra, Stafford	Dec. 15–16, 1965
Gemini-Titan 8	Armstrong, Scott	Mar. 16, 1966
Gemini-Titan 9-A	Stafford, Cernan	June 3–6, 1966
Gemini-Titan 10	Young, Collins	July 18–21, 1966
Gemini-Titan 11	Conrad, Gordon	Sept. 12–15, 1966
Gemini-Titan 12	Lovell, Aldrin	Nov. 11–15, 1966
Apollo 1	Grisson, White, Chaffee (crew killed in launchpad fire)	Jan. 27, 1967
Apollo-Saturn 7	Schirra, Eisele, Cunningham	Oct. 11–22, 1968
Apollo-Saturn 8	Borman, Lovell, Anders	Dec. 21–27, 1968
Apollo-Saturn 9	McDivitt, Scott, Schweickart	Mar. 3–13, 1969
Apollo-Saturn 10	Stafford, Young, Cernan	May 18–26, 1969
Apollo-Saturn 11	Armstrong, Collins, Aldrin	July 16–24, 1969
Apollo-Saturn 12	Conrad, Gordon, Bean	Nov. 14–24, 1969
Apollo-Saturn 13	Lovell, Swigert, Haise	April 11–17, 1970
Apollo-Saturn 14	Shepard, Roosa, Mitchell	Jan. 31–Feb. 9, 1971
Apollo-Saturn 15	Scott, Worden, Irwin	July 26–Aug. 7, 1971
Apollo-Saturn 16	Young, Mattingly, Duke	April 16–27, 1972
Apollo-Saturn 17	Cernan, Evans, Schmitt	Dec. 7–19, 1972
Skylab SL-2	Conrad, Kerwin, Weitz	May 25–June 22, 1973
Skylab SL-3	Bean, Garriott, Lousma	July 28–Sept. 25, 1973
Skylab SL-4	Carr, E. Gibson, Pogue	Nov. 16–Feb. 8, 1974

Mission		Astronaut(s)	Dates
Apollo-Soyuz Test Project (Apollo 18)		Stafford, Brand, Slayton	July 15–24, 1975
U.S. Space Shuttle Missions			
STS-1	Columbia	Young, Crippen	April 12–14, 1981
STS-2	Columbia	Engle, Truly	Nov. 12–14, 1981
STS-3	Columbia	Lousma, Fullerton	Mar. 22–30, 1982
STS-4	Columbia	Mattingly, Hartsfield	Jun. 27–July 4, 1982
STS-5	Columbia	Brand, Overmyer, Allen, Lenoir	Nov. 11–16, 1982
STS-6	Challenger	Weitz, Bobko, Peterson, Musgrave	April 4–9, 1983
STS-7	Challenger	Crippen, Hauck, Ride, Fabian, Thagard	June 18–24, 1983
STS-8	Challenger	Truly, Brandenstein, D. Gardner, Bluford, W. Thornton	Aug. 30–Sept. 5, 1983
STS-9	Columbia-Spacelab 1	Young, Shaw, Garriott, Parker, Lichtenberg, Merbold (ESA)	Nov. 28–Dec. 8, 1983
41-B	Challenger	R. Brand, R. Gibson, McCandless, McNair, Stewart	Feb. 3–11, 1984
41-C	Challenger	Crippen, Scobee, Van Hoften, G. Nelson, Hart	April 6–13, 1984
41-D	Discovery	Hartsfield, Coats, Resnik, Hawley, Mullane, C. Walker	Aug. 30–Sept. 5, 1984
41-G	Challenger	Crippen, McBride, Ride, Sullivan, Leestma, Garneau (Canada), Scully-Power	Oct. 5–13, 1984
51-A	Discovery	Hauck, D. Walker, D. Gardner, A. Fisher, Allen	Nov. 8–16, 1984
51-C	Discovery	Mattingly, Shriver, Onizuka, Buchli, Payton	Jan. 24–27, 1985
51-D	Discovery	Bobko, Williams, Seddon, Hoffman, Griggs, C. Walker, Garn	April 12–19, 1985
51-B	Challenger-Spacelab 3	Overmyer, Gregory, Lind, Thagard, W. Thornton, van den Berg (ESA), Wang	April 29–May 6, 1985
51-G	Discovery	Brandenstein, Creighton, Lucid, Fabian, Nagel, Baudry, al-Saud (Saudi Arabia)	June 17–24, 1985
51-F	Challenger-Spacelab 2	Fullerton, Bridges, Musgrave, England, Henize, Acton, Bartoe	July 29–Aug. 6, 1985
51-I	Discovery	Engle, Covey, Van Hoften, Lounge, W. Fisher	Aug. 27–Sept. 3, 1985
51-J	Atlantis	Bobko, Grabe, Hilmers, Stewart, Pailes	Oct. 3–7, 1985
61-A	Challenger-Spacelab D-1	Hartsfield, Nagel, Buchli, Bluford, Dunbar, Furrer (West Germany), Messerschmid (West Germany), Ockels (ESA)	Oct. 30–Nov. 6, 1985

Mission		*Astronaut(s)*	*Dates*
61-B	Atlantis	Shaw, O'Connor, Cleave, Spring, Ross, Neri-Vela (Mexico), C. Walker	Nov. 26–Dec. 3, 1985
61-C	Columbia	R. Gibson, Bolden, Chang-Díaz, Hawley, G. Nelson, Cenker, B. Nelson	Jan. 12–18, 1986
51-L	Challenger	Scobee, Smith, Resnik, Onizuka, McNair, Jarvis, McAuliffe (Crew died during launch)	Jan. 28, 1986
STS-26	Discovery	Hauck, Covey, G. Nelson, Hilmers, Lounge	Sept. 29–Oct. 3, 1988
STS-27	Atlantis	R. Gibson, G. Gardner, Ross, Shepherd, Mullane	Dec. 2–6, 1988
STS-29	Discovery	Coats, Blaha, Buchli, Springer, Bagian	Mar. 13–18, 1989
STS-30	Atlantis	D. Walker, Grabe, Cleave, Thagard, Lee	May 4–8, 1989
STS-28	Columbia	Shaw, Richards, Adamson, Leestma, Brown	Aug. 8–13, 1989
STS-34	Atlantis	Williams, McCulley, Lucid, Baker, Chang-Díaz	Oct. 17–23, 1989
STS-33	Discovery	Gregory, Blaha, Carter, Thornton, Musgrave	Nov. 22–27, 1989

GLOSSARY

abort To end a mission or activity prematurely (before planned completion).

Agena An upper-stage rocket booster used during Gemini missions as a docking target vehicle.

airlock An intermediate chamber between the airlessness of space and the interior pressurized quarters of a spacecraft. In space, people typically enter and exit a spacecraft by passing through an airlock; otherwise, the spacecraft would depressurize and the atmosphere would escape through the open hatch.

Apollo The NASA project that landed 12 men on the Moon between 1969 and 1972.

Apollo-Soyuz Test Project See ASTP

ASTP Apollo-Soyuz Test Project, the historic cooperative program between the United States and the USSR resulting in a joint space mission in July 1975. Two Soviets and three Americans met in space when the orbiting Apollo and Soyuz spacecraft linked up. The term "test project" was used because only one mission was planned.

astronaut Anyone who has traveled in space (over 62 miles, or 100 km in altitude, according to the standard of the Fédération Astronautique Internationale, or FAI; over 50 miles high according to U.S. Air Force standards). However, NASA gives the title of astronaut to any NASA employee who has qualified for inclusion on NASA's team of astronauts—that is, who has flown or will fly in space. Qualifications have varied depending on the program and the mission requirements. NASA's group of astronauts does not include payload specialists from outside NASA who have flown on U.S. space flights, e.g., Senator Jake Garn or Loren Acton of Lockheed. In this book we have used the FAI standard, however.

Atlas rocket The rocket that powered the launches of Project Mercury missions. Originally designed as an ICBM (a military missile).

ballistic Describes the flight path that returns a projectile, such as a missile, spacecraft or bullet, to Earth along a curved path after the thrust or propelling force has ended. Early spacecraft such as Mercury and Vostok traveled along ballistic trajectories.

booster In a multistage rocket, any of the rockets that provide the early stages of propulsion, including the initial stage that provides power for the launching and initial part of the flight.

Cape Canaveral Location of NASA's Kennedy Space Center and the Air Force station from which all Mercury and Gemini missions were launched as well as, to this day, most unmanned missions. Called Cape Kennedy between 1963 and 1973.

cargo bay The area of a spacecraft (most commonly the U.S. Shuttle) used to transport equipment, experiments and so on. Satellites to be launched during a Shuttle mission, for example, are carried in the cargo bay, located behind the crew quarters.

CM The Command Module, one of the three main parts of the Apollo spacecraft. Shaped like a cone, it contained the crew quarters, and was the only portion of the spacecraft that returned to Earth at the completion of a mission.

combustion Rapid oxidation or burning.

cosmonaut Name given to those who have flown or will fly aboard a Soviet space flight.

CSM The Command/Service Module (Command Module and Service Module combined) of the Apollo spacecraft.

DM Docking Module, a section of a spacecraft (such as Skylab) that enables docking or joining with another spacecraft.

docking When two spacecraft connect or "link up" with each other in orbit.

docking adaptor An apparatus that makes it possible for one spacecraft to link up with another.

EDT Eastern Daylight Time (one hour ahead of EST), the official time used for all launches made during summer months from Kennedy Space Center in Florida.

electromagnetic radiation Waves or rays created by variations in magnetic and electric fields—including radio waves, infrared, visible light, ultraviolet, x-rays and gamma rays.

electromagnetic spectrum The entire range of

electromagnetic radiation from gamma rays (the shortest wavelength) to radio waves (the longest) and including visible light.

EST Eastern Standard Time, the official time used for all launches made during the winter months from Kennedy Space Center (located in Florida).

EVA Extravehicular activity—a space walk (outside the protection of a spacecraft).

exhaust gas The stream or jet of gases expelled by burning rocket fuel.

fusion The process of combining two substances by melting.

gamma ray telescope A special telescope used by astronomers to detect gamma rays emitted by objects in space (such as galaxies and quasars). Gamma rays, which are extremely short-wavelength electromagnetic radiation, cannot penetrate the Earth's atmosphere, so they can be observed only from space (for example, from a satellite or spacecraft).

Gemini NASA's second manned space project, lasting from 1965–1966. The Gemini spacecraft carried two astronauts on each mission.

geostationary orbit A special circular geosynchronous orbit (see Glossary entry) at the equator. From the Earth a satellite in geostationary orbit seems to hover motionless in one spot above the Earth although it is actually traveling as fast as the Earth is rotating, one revolution every 24 hours.

geosynchronous orbit A special orbit 22,300 miles above the Earth, where a satellite's movement is synchronized (*-synchronous*) with the Earth (*geo-*).

ICBM An inter-continental ballistic missile. A military rocket carrying a nuclear warhead and designed to travel at least 3,000 miles. The rocket power of the ICBM formed the foundation for both U.S. and Soviet space programs.

high-resolution imaging The use of highly sensitive instruments (such as a camera) to produce close-up images. Cameras aboard certain military satellites, for example, can reportedly photograph areas on the Earth's surface just a few inches across.

infrared Radiation lying just outside the visible spectrum at the red end, with wavelengths shorter than radio waves. Infrared radiation cannot be seen with the naked eye, but infrared radiation from many stars and galaxies can be detected by an infrared telescope such as the one carried aboard IRAS (Infrared Astronomical Satellite) in 1983.

JPL Jet Propulsion Laboratory, in Pasadena, California. A NASA research laboratory, transferred from Army jurisdiction to NASA in 1958, and operated in conjunction with the California Institute of Technology. JPL managed the (unmanned) Ranger and Surveyor missions to the Moon, as well as many later planetary missions such as Pioneer missions to Jupiter and Saturn and Voyager missions to Jupiter, Saturn, Uranus and Neptune.

JSC Johnson Space Center, the NASA center at Clear Lake, Texas, near Houston. Previously known as the Manned Spacecraft Center, this site houses NASA Mission Control, which manages all manned space flights after lift-off from Cape Canaveral Air Force Station (Mercury, Gemini and most unmanned missions) or from Kennedy Space Center (Apollo missions and, later, Skylab and Shuttle missions).

KSC Kennedy Space Center, the NASA center on Merritt Island in Florida. All Apollo missions were launched from KSC (as well as, later, all Skylab and Shuttle missions).

LANDSAT Name given to a series of Earth observation satellites.

lift-off Ascent of a spacecraft from the launchpad (at least two inches).

liquid propellant A fuel, such as liquid oxygen (LOX), that burns in a liquid state.

LM The Lunar Module, one of the three main parts of the Apollo spacecraft, used to land astronauts on the Moon.

materials processing Manufacturing or transforming substances, an activity of interest in space, since, for example, near-perfect ball bearings and crystals can be created in the weightless environment of space.

Mercury The NASA project that included the first U.S. manned missions into space.

Mercury Seven The first seven U.S. astronauts, chosen to participate in the Mercury missions.

Mir The new-generation Soviet space station launched February 20, 1986. The name means "peace."

mission specialist An astronaut on a U.S. Space Shuttle crew who is responsible for some aspect of mission operations (pilot training not required).

MMU Manned maneuvering unit, a special jet-propelled backpack that enables Shuttle astronauts to work without a tether to the spacecraft during EVA. First used by Bruce McCandless and Robert Stewart during STS-41B in 1984, when McCandless flew the distance of half a football field from the spacecraft.

multistage rocket Several rockets fired in combination to achieve greater heights.

NASA National Aeronautics and Space Administration, the U.S. space agency.

neutral buoyancy tank A very large "swimming pool," filled with water, used for testing equipment and procedures for use in space. By using weights that correct for the tendency of objects and people to float, astronauts and technicians swimming underwater in this tank can simulate the weightlessness of space.

nozzle The opening at the rear of a rocket or thruster engine through which exhaust gases flow.

payload Anything that's not part of the functioning of a rocket or spacecraft but is transported by it to carry out a purpose or mission; cargo.

payload specialist A specialist (not usually employed by NASA) who goes into space aboard the Space Shuttle to perform specific scientific experiments or other work.

PDT Pacific Daylight Time (one hour ahead of standard time), the official time used for all Shuttle landings made during the summer months at Edwards Air Force Base in California.

projectile Any object propelled forward by a force. For example, a bullet or a spacecraft.

propulsion A force that propels, or pushes, an object forward.

Proton booster The Soviet "D-class" launch vehicle, designed to lift heavy loads such as the *Salyut* and *Mir* space stations and the first Soviet booster not developed directly from a military rocket. Introduced in July 1965, it is an enlarged version of the smaller "A-class" booster (used to launch all three Sputnik satellites, as well as Vostok, Voskhod, Soyuz and Progress missions). The USSR is currently promoting the Proton launcher for use by the rest of the world as a commercial launch vehicle.

PST Pacific Standard Time, the official time used for all Shuttle landings made during the winter months at Edwards Air Force Base.

rendezvous When two spacecraft in orbit are brought almost close enough together to touch.

retrofire Firing rockets in the opposite direction from the direction of flight to slow a spacecraft (a procedure used during reentry).

retropack A system of auxiliary rockets (retrorockets) on a spacecraft, used to reduce speed by firing in the opposite direction from the direction of travel.

retrorockets Rockets used to slow the speed of a spacecraft. They are fired in the opposite direction from the direction of flight ("retro-" or backward) to bring the spacecraft back into the atmosphere.

Salyut The name given the first seven Soviet space stations. The first Salyut was launched April 19, 1971. Salyut 7, launched April 19, 1982, was "retired" though still orbiting when the Mir space station was launched in 1986. The name means "salute," honoring Soviet cosmonaut Yuri Gagarin, the first human in space.

Saturn rocket A powerful, giant rocket designed to send Apollo missions to the Moon.

simulator Any device that makes it possible to practice an activity outside the usual environment and without using the actual equipment (for example, a flight simulator). For space missions, underwater simulators (in neutral buoyancy tanks) have proven highly useful to both Soviet and American manned programs. To simulate weightlessness, a mock-up spacecraft can be placed in a huge underwater tank where swimmers fitted with weights can achieve "neutral buoyancy"—they neither sink nor float to the surface. Astronauts and cosmonauts train in such simulators, and ground crews often help during missions by trying out solutions to problems in an underwater simulator.

Skylab U.S. space station, which was in service for two years, manned by three teams of astronauts in 1973 and 1974. Unmanned for the following five years, it crashed to Earth in 1979.

SM The Service Module, one of the three main parts of the Apollo spacecraft. Cylindrical in shape, it contained fuel, supplies and engines.

solar array A panel (often wing-shaped) of solar cells used for power, for example, aboard Soyuz, Skylab and Mir.

solar cell A device used to convert rays from the Sun directly into electrical power.

solar flare A sudden short-lived outburst of energy from a small area of the Sun's surface.

solid fuel A fuel, such as gunpowder, that is a solid (as opposed to being in a liquid or a gaseous state).

sounding rocket A rocket used to obtain information about the atmosphere.

Soyuz A Soviet spacecraft originally designed to carry three cosmonauts. Its name, meaning "union," indicates its main mission, to provide transportation to and from a space station, where it could dock during missions aboard the station. The descendants of this spacecraft, the Soyuz TM series, are still being flown today.

spaceplane A vehicle that can take off horizontally from Earth, achieve speeds many times faster than sound, fly above the atmosphere to space and then return and land like an airplane.

space suit A suit equipped with life-support provisions (such as oxygen, temperature regulation, pressurization, protection against radiation and so on) to allow the wearer to function in space outside the spacecraft; an EVA suit.

spationaut Name given by the French to their astronauts.

speed of sound At 32 degrees F (0 degrees C) the speed of sound in air is about 760 mph (332 meters per second).

Sputnik The first artificial satellite, launched by the USSR on October 4, 1957. The name means, roughly, "traveling companion," and two more were also later launched.

suborbital Describes a flight that does not make an orbit around the Earth, such as Alan Shepard's Mercury flight.

subsonic Slower than the speed of sound.

supersonic Faster than the speed of sound.

thrust The push forward caused in reaction to a high-speed jet of fluid or gases discharged in the opposite direction from a rocket's nozzle.

thrusters Rocket engines, especially those used for maneuvering a spacecraft.

trajectory The path traveled by a flying object, such as a rocket or spacecraft.

transfer module An airlock through which one can enter or leave a spacecraft.

Tyuratam The Soviet launch site, located on the broad, flat steppes of Central Asia, about 200 miles from the town of Baikonur (the name often used by the Soviets for the launch site).

ultraviolet Radiation having a wavelength shorter than visible light (just beyond the violet end of the visible spectrum and therefore can't be seen by the naked eye) and longer than x-rays.

upper stage In a multistage rocket, a booster rocket that takes over after the first-stage rocket has burned its fuel.

venting out Expelling a gas.

Voskhod A modified Soviet Vostok spacecraft, used for two manned missions in 1964–65. Its name means "ascent."

Vostok The first manned Soviet spacecraft. Its name means "east."

x-ray telescope An instrument used to collect and measure x-ray radiation from objects in space. Many nearby stars and other astronomical objects emit x-rays, but one example is the well-known Crab nebula, left over from an ancient supernova.

SUGGESTIONS FOR FURTHER READING

Aldrin, Buzz, and Malcolm McConnell. *Men from Earth*. New York: Bantam, 1989.

Aldrin, Edwin E., Jr. [Buzz]. *Return to Earth*. New York: Random House, 1973.

Armstrong, Neil, Michael Collins, and Edwin E. Aldrin, Jr., et al. *First on the Moon*. Boston: Little, Brown and Co., Inc., 1970.

Ash, Brian, Ed. *The Visual Encyclopedia of Science Fiction*. New York: Harmony Books, 1977.

Associated Press. *Moments in Space*. New York: Gallery Books, 1986.

Baker, David. *The History of Manned Space Flight, Revised Edition*. New York: Crown Publishers, Inc., 1982.

————. *The Rocket: The History and Development of Rocket & Missile Technology*. New York: Crown Publishers, Inc., 1978.

Belew, Leland F. *Skylab, Our First Space Station*. Washington, DC: NASA, 1977.

Benford, Timothy B., and Brian Wilkes. *The Space Program Quiz & Fact Book*. New York: Harper & Row, 1985.

Bergaust, Erik. *Reaching for the Stars*. New York: Doubleday, 1960.

————. *Rocket City, USA*. New York: Macmillan, 1963.

Bond, Peter. *Heroes in Space: From Gagarin to Challenger*. New York: Basil Blackwell, Inc., 1987.

Borman, Frank, with Robert J. Serling. *Countdown: An Autobiography*. New York: Silver Arrow Books, 1988.

Braun, Wernher von, et al. *Space Travel: A History*. An update (and Fourth Edition) of *History of Rocketry & Space Travel*. New York: Harper & Row, 1985.

Cassutt, Michael. *Who's Who in Space: The First 25 Years*. Boston: G. K. Hall & Co., 1987.

Clark, Phillip. *The Soviet Manned Space Program: An Illustrated History of the Men, the Missions, and the Spacecraft*. New York: Orion Books, 1988.

Collins, Michael. *Carrying the Fire: An Astronaut's Journey*. New York: Farrar, Straus & Giroux, 1974.

————. *Liftoff: The Story of America's Adventure in Space*. New York: Grove Press, 1988.

Cooper, Henry S. F. Jr. *A House in Space*. New York: Holt, Rinehart and Winston, 1976.

Cortright, Edgar M., Ed. *Apollo Expeditions to the Moon*. Washington, D. C.: NASA, 1975.

Dewaard, E. John and Nancy. *History of NASA: America's Voyage to the Stars*. New York: Exeter Books, 1984.

Gatland, Kenneth. *Space Diary*. New York: Crescent Books, 1989.

————, et al. *The Illustrated Encyclopedia of Space Technology: A Comprehensive History of Space Exploration*. New York: Harmony Books, 1981.

Grissom, Betty, and Henry Still. *Starfall*. New York: Crowell, 1974.

Grissom, Virgil I. *Gemini: A Personal Account of Man's Venture into Space*. New York: Macmillan, 1968.

Gurney, Gene, and Jeff Forte. *Space Shuttle Log: The First 25 Flights*. Foreword by James M. Beggs, former NASA Administrator and Preface by Milton A. Silveira, former NASA Chief Engineer. Blue Ridge Summit, PA: Aero (A Division of Tab Books), 1988.

Hart, Douglas. *The Encyclopedia of Soviet Spacecraft*. New York: Exeter Books, 1987.

Hurt, Harry, III. *For All Mankind*. New York: Atlantic Monthly Press, 1988.

Johnson, Nicholas L. *Handbook of Soviet Manned Space Flight*. San Diego: Univelt, Inc., 1980.

Kerrod, Robin. *The Illustrated History of NASA*. New York: Gallery Books, 1986.

Lehman, Milton. *This High Man: The Life of Robert H. Goddard*. New York: Farrar, Straus & Co., 1963.

Ley, Willy. *Rockets, Missiles and Space Travel*. New York: Viking, 1961.

McAleer, Neil. *The Omni Space Almanac*. New York: World Almanac, 1987.

McDougall, Walter A. *... the Heavens and the Earth: A Political History of the Space Age*. New York: Basic Books, Inc., 1985.

Nicholls, Peter, Ed. *The Science Fiction Encyclopedia*. Garden City, New York: Dolphin Books, 1979.

Oberg, James E. *Red Star in Orbit: The Inside Story of Soviet Failures and Triumphs in Space*. New York: Random House, 1981.

———, and Alcestis R. Oberg. *Pioneering Space: Living on the Next Frontier*. Foreword by Isaac Asimov. New York: McGraw-Hill, 1986.

Ordway, Frederick L., III, and Mitchell R. Sharpe. *The Rocket Team*. New York: Thomas Y. Crowell, 1979.

Pioneering the Space Frontier: The Report of the National Commission on Space. (Paine Commission Report.) New York: Bantam, 1986.

Report to the President by the Presidential Commission on the Space Shuttle Challenger Accident. (Rogers Commission Report.) Washington, DC, 1986.

Schirra, Walter M., Jr., with Richard N. Billings. *Schirra's Space*. Boston: Quinlan Press, 1988.

Shepard, Alan B., Jr.; Virgil I. Grissom; John H. Glenn, Jr.; M. Scott Carpenter; Walter M. Schirra, Jr.; L. Gordon Cooper, Jr.; and Donald K. Slayton. *We Seven*. New York: Simon & Schuster, 1962.

Silvestri, Goffredo, et al. *Quest for Space: Man's Greatest Adventure—The Facts, the Machines, the Technology*. Trans. Simon Pleasance. New York: Crescent Books, 1987.

Smolders, Peter. *Soviets in Space*. Trans. Marian Powell. New York: Taplinger Publishing Co., Inc., 1974.

Swenson, Loyd S., Jr., et al. *This New Ocean: A History of Project Mercury*. The NASA Historical Series. Washington, D.C.: NASA, 1966.

Tsiolkovsky, K.E. *Selected Works*. Trans. G. Yankovsky. Moscow: Mir Publishers, 1968.

Williams, Beryl, and Samuel Epstein. *The Rocket Piioneers on the Road to Space*. New York: Julian Messner, Inc., 1955.

Wolfe, Tom. *The Right Stuff*. New York: Farrar, Straus & Giroux, 1979.

Yeager, Chuck, and Leo Janos. *Yeager—An Autobiography*. New York: Bantam Books, 1985.

Yenne, Bill. *The Astronauts: The First 25 Years of Manned Space Flight*. New York: Exeter Books, 1986.

———. *The Encyclopedia of U.S. Spacecraft*. New York: Exeter Books, 1985.

Periodicals:

Ad Astra. Washington, DC: National Space Society.

Air & Space. Washington, DC: Smithsonian Institution.

Final Frontier. Minneapolis, MN: Final Frontier Publishing Co.

Spaceflight. London: British Interplanetary Society.

INDEX